The Fraternity Leader

Patrick Daley

DEDICATION

For the Jungleman - Jamesaroo

SPECIAL THANKS

To the Mooster – the book is better with your input.

Thank you!

CONTENTS

INTRODUCTION

Thank you for purchasing my book. I know it will help you become the leader you want to be and help your fraternity in the process.

Before we start though, I'd like to share a little information about me:

I was initiated into Pi Lambda Phi Fraternity at North Carolina State University in the fall of 1997. I joined a very young chapter. I was initiated the weekend after we were chartered, and was able to see the chapter grow from its infancy.

I would go on to become the president of my chapter for two years as well as the IFC president of the university. I was elected to be the Undergraduate Representative to Pi Lambda Phi's International Executive Council. These organizations thrived under my leadership, and I was recognized with the following awards:

- Brother of the Year – NC State University Chapter of Pi Lambda Phi Fraternity
- NC State University Fraternity Man of the Year
- Rafer Johnson Upsilon Achievement Award – presented to the most outstanding brother nationally in Pi Lambda Phi Fraternity

After graduation I took a job as a robotics engineer for an Italian robotics company. However, when the Iraq War broke out, I decided to join the United States Air Force.

As an Air Force officer I deployed to the Middle East twice. That is where the idea of this book and thefraternityadvisor.com started. I started to compile the things I had learned as a successful fraternity leader during my free time in Balad, Iraq. I knew I could offer a lot to the Greek community, and I envisioned this as a way I would be able to give back.

Unfortunately, I let my writing sit for a few years. I had lost my passion for fraternity due to being so far removed from my chapter. Fortunately, a chance encounter with an undergraduate brother in my fraternity reignited my desire to give back to the Greek community that gave me so much.

I launched the site in the summer of 2009 and it has been a huge success. Over a million people have read my columns, and it is very rewarding to think that I have been able to help so many people improve their fraternities.

I developed this book as an ebook at the end of 2010. Due to its success, I decided to have The Fraternity Leader published.

Again, I sincerely appreciate you purchasing the book, and I welcome any feedback you can give. My hope is that this book becomes a favorite resource for fraternity brothers everywhere.

Best of luck in your journey as a fraternity leader. I hope you get as much out of your fraternity experience as I did.

Fraternally,

Pat

info@thefraternityadvisor.com

Facebook.com/Thefraternityadvisor

Twitter.com/thefratadvisor

1 - RECRUITMENT MADE EASY

Here is a typical recruitment strategy in a typical chapter:

Let's stalk freshman the first week of school. Let's get them to the fraternity house, get them drunk, and then try to get them to join our fraternity for life!

Who cares that these guys don't really know what fraternity is all about. Hell, they don't even know where their classes are. If we can trick them into signing their bid, then we'll have them forever!

It is frightening that most of our chapters are built on this strategy, and it is no wonder that recruitment numbers are down across the country. There has to be a better way. Fortunately, there is...

This chapter lays out a systematic method for recruiting guys. This approach minimizes the inconvenience to the brothers and increases your chances of recruiting a solid class. It turns recruitment into a simple numbers game, and makes it easy to build on your success semester after semester.

The Recruitment Percentage

What percentage of the guys who attend your rush events end up becoming new members?

This number is the foundation for your entire recruitment program. We'll call it your recruitment percentage (RP) for the rest of this chapter.

If you know your fraternity's RP, then you can focus your efforts on two things:

1) Increasing the number of guys who attend your rush events (growing your list)

2) Increasing the percentage of guys who join

It really is that simple. Either recruit more guys, or get a higher percentage of guys to join.

Let me explain with a couple examples.

You know that your chapter gets about 25% of the guys who rush to join. You know that because you do a good job tracking those numbers from previous semesters. That means your RP is 25%.

You know you will get 100 guys to rush your house this fall. That means you should get 25 guys to join.

But let's say that you want a larger new member class. There are really only two things you can do to grow your class.

First, you can recruit more guys. If your RP is 25%, and you want a 50 man new member class, then you need to rush 200 guys.

Or, you can do the second option, increase your RP. If you can increase your RP to 50%, then you can get 50 guys to join from that same 100 guys rushing.

This systematic method of recruitment will get your fraternity to focus on two variables – increasing the number of guys rushing or increasing the percentage of guys joining. This will simplify your recruitment, and increase your chances of success.

Let's dig deeper into these two areas where you will need to focus...

Increase the Number of Guys Who Attend Your Rush Events – Grow Your List

The very first thing you need to do when you start planning for recruitment is make a list of potential guys that you want to join your fraternity. This will help you focus your efforts and will become the foundation for your recruitment period. This is a very critical part of this step, and its importance cannot be overstated.

When you start to build your list, build it with the people you already know.

All too often chapters will waste their time trying to find complete strangers to join. That just doesn't make sense. It takes time to meet people, then it takes a lot more effort to make them your friends to the point where they will want to join your fraternity. Since your rush period is only two weeks (typically), you really don't have the time to make that many new friends. That is why you need to be meeting new people and growing your list all year long.

So the next obvious question is where do you find guys to put on the list? Really, there are only three places to look. You either know them from home, you meet them at school, or they are recommended to you. That is it. Let's dive deeper into each category.

First, your main focus needs to be recruiting guys from your hometown. All of us have friends in high school that were a year or two younger than us, and chose to follow in our footsteps. These guys are prime targets for recruitment. You need to understand you have instant credibility because you are attending the college that they will be attending.

You need to use that edge to your advantage. It is important that you reach out to these guys before they arrive on campus, most typically the summer after their senior year in high school. If you are a true friend, you will be eager to help them with their transition from high school to college regardless of if they want to join a fraternity.

When this situation presents itself, it isn't a good idea to give them the full-court fraternity pitch until they arrive on campus. They aren't going to understand, and you most likely will turn them off to the idea.

That is not to say that you shouldn't talk about it though. Fraternity is an important part of your college life. It would be strange if you didn't talk about it. Your goal is to earn the trust of your friend so you can get them to a rush event in the fall. You will have plenty of opportunities to give them the sales pitch later.

If you play your cards right, you will be able to seek your friend out the day he arrives on campus. This will be a hectic day, but you have to make seeing him your number one priority. He will inevitably have questions, and as his trusted confidant you should provide the answers. If you have done enough to develop the relationship, you should be able to plant the seed for him to attend a rush event.

The beauty of this method is that if you can get your friend to rush, you will invariably get a few of his friends to rush as well. He will have a roommate, and he will have a few friends from home. You just have to get one guy out to get several. Be sure to add all these guys to your list!

The second place to find guys to rush is in the dorms. While it is important to keep the fraternity house completely rented out, it is just as important to have some guys living in the dorms. The dorms will always be a fertile ground for recruitment, especially for brothers who live there.

Truthfully, there is no easier way to recruit guys than by being an RA in a freshman dorm. I was exactly that for two years, and found more than my share of guys. It was really quite simple.

You earn instant credibility because you are the first person that the recruit meets when he arrives on campus. You gain instant credibility from his parents because you will have met them the day their son moved-in. They figure that you must have something going for you since you made it through the university's RA screening process. The ground work is set, and all you have to do is ask him to attend a rush event.

The final way to find guys to recruit is by recommendation. It really doesn't matter where the recommendation is coming from. What matters is that you take advantage of it.

The easiest recommendation is a legacy. It is absolutely essential that you take advantage of this connection. While this would seem like a no-brainer, you would be surprised at how many guys fall through the cracks. When my younger brother arrived on campus a couple semesters after I had graduated, not one guy from my fraternity tried to recruit him. I was shocked. I gave my fraternity all his information before he set foot on campus, and told them that he would be expecting the call. The call never came. Imagine my disappointment.

Recommendations can come in different forms than legacies. Be sure to ask your alumni for recommendations. Be sure to ask your friends in sororities. It takes a couple of minutes to email your contacts asking them if they would recommend anyone for membership. If you even get one name back, then it will be well worth the effort.

All the other methods are a waste of time. Fraternity recruitment too often employs the shotgun approach which yields minimal success. If you target your efforts to the areas mentioned above, your fraternity will have a tremendously successful recruitment.

To be honest, I know a lot of chapters are good at mining guys these three ways. Note that this is just half the battle.

All these names need to be collected and tracked in your list. That way the chapter knows how many guys they are recruiting. The list also enables a rush chair to assign responsibilities to each brother, which makes sure that none of these guys fall through the cracks.

It is important that the recruitment chair is keeping up with the list and making sure that every brother is contributing to grow it. Without this critical document, there is no structure to your program.

Increasing the Percentage of Guys who Join

Now that you have your list of guys who are potential new members, you need to focus on getting the highest percentage of those guys to join.

Most fraternities center their efforts on rush events. Often, there will be a rush event scheduled every night for the first two weeks of the semester. Some brothers will look at rush as a chore, and it will be like pulling teeth to get them motivated to recruit. This will obviously hurt your recruitment efforts.

Because of this, it is pretty obvious that rush shouldn't be a drag. Ideally, the recruitment chair needs to set up the recruitment events as if they were brotherhood events. These need to be events that the brothers *want* to go to. If the brothers are excited about going to the events because they will be a lot of fun, this will leave a great impression on the guys you are recruiting.

Having brothers who are having a good time and are motivated to recruit will also have a tremendous impact on your RP. But getting the brothers motivated is just part of the battle.

You also need to eliminate the reasons why guys won't join your fraternity. Essentially this boils down to answering the following questions that you know the potential new member is going to ask:

Q. What is the cost of joining a fraternity?

A. I would tell the recruit exactly what the new member dues and brotherhood dues are. Then I would explain where every penny went and why that expense exists. The critical question the recruit wants to be answered is if he is getting enough out of the fraternity to justify the cost. Explain to him the benefit of each expense. For example, make sure he realizes that because all the brothers pool their money together they are able to afford a great house and a great social program. These are two of the many things you can't have unless you are in a fraternity.

Finances are probably the number one excuse guys use when they don't want to join a fraternity. Many times though it is just an excuse for covering up the real reason.

That being said, if your chapter is smart, you will eliminate your new member dues through fundraisers. This way, you will be able to explain to the new members that they are able to join the chapter without an initial, unexpected financial commitment.

Then, if they decide they want to be brothers in the fraternity, they will be expected to pay their dues as an initiated brother. If they don't, they will be able to quit the new member program with no financial loss.

Remember that not everyone is cut out to be in a fraternity. It is best to be honest and up front with guys about the financial commitments of a brother. The last thing you want is to have a brother on your hands who does not meet their financial obligations.

Q. Does your chapter haze?

A. If your chapter does haze, then you need to reevaluate what your chapter is all about. Hazing is the most damaging thing you can do to your chapter because it kills camaraderie with new members and de-motivates brothers.

To answer the question, I would explain that my chapter has a no hazing policy. I would explain though that during their new member period, they wouldn't do anything that they wouldn't want to do in front of their family.

However, I would explain to them that while they won't be hazed, that doesn't mean that the new member program will be easy. Like anything worth having in life, it will take hard work and effort to make it through the new member period. They must remember that every event in the new member program has a purpose. Sometimes they may not understand that purpose at the time. One day though, it will all click.

This moment is hard to explain, and everyone has it at a different time. When a new member has that moment, he will understand the reason for everything he has been taught in the new member program.

If they work through the program as a unified new member class, their efforts will be rewarded by a great college experience.

Q. What are the time commitments?

A. Again, you need to be honest when answering this question. Let them know what they are expected to attend. Remind them that even though this will be an extra commitment, this is something they will look forward to doing. New member nights are designed to be a lot of fun, and will often be the highlight of the week.

In addition, if they didn't have these new member commitments, they would probably end up wasting time watching TV instead of enjoying the things that college life has to offer.

The most important thing I would explain when this question is asked is that the new member period is a probationary period. They really don't know the brothers, and the brothers really don't know them. If the recruit feels that the chapter isn't a good fit, they can quit the new member program with no hard feelings.

By letting the recruit know the commitment isn't permanent, he will become more willing to take a chance and try it out. If it doesn't work out, at least he'll have the knowledge that he tried and it wasn't the right fit for him.

Q. Will joining hurt my grades?

A. I would always tell the perspective member that it is up to them how they perform in school, and fraternity is really irrelevant in this regard. If they are looking for an excuse for not performing well in class, they will be everywhere. However, if they are dedicated to their studies, they will perform well regardless of their extracurricular activities.

Remind the recruit that there are brothers who are excellent students. Also, let them know that the success of the chapter is partially judged on GPA, especially the new member class GPA. In fact, most chapters are punished by the university if the new member class GPA is sub-par. A chapter would be foolish to do anything that would hurt their new members academically.

Also, explain the academic benefits of joining a chapter. I would always explain how I would seek tutoring from a certain brother before every math test. This guy was super smart, and was always available to help me because I was a brother.

I would finally explain that brothers will often conduct group study sessions for younger members for common classes. Joining a brotherhood isn't just something that is said, it should be backed up with action and common concern for each other's success. This is especially true for academic success.

Q. My parents won't approve

A. This is another common excuse. You need to ask them why their parents won't approve. They will probably give you a selection from these questions. If this really becomes a hold up, offer to have someone from the chapter, or your alumni advisor, speak to their parents.

If you are the right person to speak to them, then by all means do so. Most times they will not take you up on the offer, but if they do, at least the parents will respect that you are concerned enough about their opinion to call.

When you do speak to the parents, be sure to have good answers for the questions you know they are going to ask. Parents are always looking out for the best interests of the child. They want to make sure that their kid is not joining Animal House. Let them know that you are a respectable group of guys. Let them know about the chapter's accomplishments.

For example, if you do a lot of volunteer work for charity, tell them. If your chapter GPA is really good, tell them. If you have brothers who achieved after graduating from the college and chapter, tell them. At this point you are rushing the parent. Be sure you put your best foot forward.

Q. I think I want to wait until the spring semester

A. This is a very common statement, and to be honest, one that makes a lot of sense for most people. Most of the time, this is an excuse that masks the real reason. It is an easy way to say no without saying no.

Remind them that they can wait, but if they really want to join, why would they wait six months? Life is full of opportunities that present themselves at awkward times. This is obviously one of those awkward times. By not taking advantage of this opportunity though, they will miss out of six months of great times and great memories that they can never get back.

Also, joining in the fall semester of freshman year is the best time to become a new member. For one, everything is new and they don't have any preconceived notions of how things should be. This allows them to make an honest evaluation of the organization they are looking to join. The fall new member class is always bigger than the spring new member class, which equals a lot more fun and energy. There is no time like the present. No one knows what tomorrow holds.

Q. Do I have to live in the house?

A. The thought of living in the house does not make sense to people who aren't in a fraternity. Most chapter houses are not very clean, and probably don't create the best academic environment.

It is important that you don't force a recruit into a corner and tell them they have to live in the house at some point. If your chapter has a mandatory policy, you might think about revising it. While it is essential that the house remains full, it is also stupid to have a policy in place that scares recruits away.

My chapter always had a policy that the brother did not have to live in the house, but their brotherhood dues were a little higher. I would explain to a recruit that while they may not understand the appeal of living in the house now, they probably will in the future.

The chapter house is the center of the fraternity, and by living there they will always be in touch with what is going on.

I would also always point out the brothers who were great brothers but never lived in the house as proof that it isn't required.

Another way that brothers can contribute is by living in the house during the summer. There are always plenty of empty rooms in the house when school is not in session. It can have a big impact on chapter finances if brothers who don't live in the house during the school year decide to live there those few months.

Your chapter needs to be committed to answering these questions for more reasons than getting a guy to join. These questions reflect the health of your fraternity. If these are reasons why guys won't join, then maybe these are reasons why your brothers aren't as happy with the chapter as they could be.

Focus on providing answers to these issues, and your RP will improve as a result.

Finally, and most importantly, you need to give them a reason to join. Sure having fun is important, as is eliminating the reasons why they won't join. Neither of these will matter if there aren't enough compelling reasons why they would want to join your chapter.

In my experience, there are only six reasons why guys join fraternities. Figuring out which category your potential new member falls into can be difficult, but extremely beneficial. Realize that most people actually join because of a combination of the six.

The first and most common reason why guys join fraternities is because they are looking for acceptance. Most guys who will be rushing your fraternity are freshman who have just recently stepped foot onto a college campus. They have left behind everything they have ever known, especially their comfort zone. It is natural for a guy to be looking for a place to fit in. Your fraternity provides that opportunity.

To gain their confidence, you have to make them feel like they are part of the group. The first step towards accomplishing this is the simplest. You must remember the recruit's name and make sure they remember yours. Think about it, the recruit is going to be in a room full of strangers. He is going to get names mixed up and is going to feel out of place. It will appeal to his self worth if you make it a point to refer to him by his name. Doing so makes the recruit feel like he is accepted and remembered.

Then, you must always remind the recruit of your name when you speak to him. Not only is that the classy thing to do, but it gives the recruit an opportunity to tell you that he remembered who you are. It doesn't matter if that is a white lie or not. By saying that he remembers you, he is acknowledging a relationship exists.

If enough brothers take the time to do this, he will definitely feel like the fraternity has accepted him. If you are really looking to score big, make sure the girls who are around do the same thing. Think of the impression it will make on a freshman if an attractive, older girl strikes up a conversation with him and knows who he is. It doesn't matter if the girl is a brother's girlfriend or sister. It will leave a huge impression.

The second reason why guys join fraternities is as a resume builder. Appealing to this crowd is easy. Go to thefraternityadvisor.com and get all the impressive stats on fraternity men. You know the ones I am talking about. The ones that say a crazy percentage of the Fortune 500 CEOs and members of Congress are Greek. That is good information to share, and is a good first step.

The next step would be to tell them a story of how a brother has used their fraternity experience to get a job. The story I would always tell recruits is how I got my first job. I would explain that when I applied for my first job with IBM, I had no real engineering experience. Truth be told, I didn't have very good grades either. The only thing I could sell them on is my leadership ability. Fortunately, my fraternity experience provided me great examples of how my leadership transformed an organization.

I explained how my efforts as president led to our chapter GPA increasing for four straight semesters. I explained that I organized an event that raised $5,000 for the Jimmy V Foundation for Cancer Research. I explained that I had to make the tough call on holding brothers accountable for their actions and the positive results that occurred as a result. I then summarized by explaining the awards I received as a result of my accomplishments.

Make sure the type of recruit that is looking to build his resume realizes that he will be building a network that will help him later in life. Make sure he realizes that this network of brothers who will be able to assist him in getting a job once he graduates. If your recruit is really looking for resume fodder, give him what he wants.

The third reason why guys join a fraternity is for the leadership experience. These are the guys you want in your fraternity. They are the type A personalities that form the backbone of all chapters. These are the guys who are going to put in the long hours to make your fraternity great. You need to make sure these guys know that the leadership opportunities they seek are out there.

I would always relate this back to fraternity elections. Most young guys believe you have to be elected to a position to be a leader. While this couldn't be further from the truth, it isn't a topic worth debating during rush.

Start by explaining to them when the next election is, and what positions they would be expected to fill. With these guys it is a good idea to develop a road map that would lead them to becoming president of the fraternity. That is really their goal, so explain to them how it could happen.

Continue by explaining that as a freshman they can hold a position like athletics director or fund raising chair. While these aren't glamorous positions, they are definitely important and great stepping stones. They are also crucial to the fraternity's success.

Then, explain the impact that the recruit could have if he has a couple great fund raising events, or if the team performed well in intramurals. Not many events have a bigger impact on the health of a fraternity than a successful fund raising event. Everyone who has ever been in a fraternity realizes that the most points in fraternity athletic standings come from participation. If the guy can get brothers to raise some money or show up to most athletic events, he will have a profound positive impact on the fraternity. He will also show his ability to manage and lead in the process.

If he is successful there, he will be in line for a more prestigious committee chair or an executive board position his sophomore year. I would explain that he would still need to make a difference in whatever position he takes. Holding a position is never good enough. What matters is what the individual accomplishes in that position. If the guy could find his way into becoming the social chair or onto the executive board, he will have great experiences that will help him in his goal of becoming president.

From there, explain to him that his year is going to be his junior year. Seniors rarely make good presidents because they are too busy trying to graduate. Letting him know that he is two small jumps from the big chair should be very appealing. Let him know that you can see the potential in him (remember that you are selling him on the idea and appealing to his ego) and you expect big things from him when he gets there.

The fourth reason guys join fraternities is because their friends are joining and they don't want to be left behind. Let's face it, a lot of guys are followers, not leaders. There is nothing wrong with that, and you need these guys in your fraternity. To get these guys you need to make sure you can convince the leader of the group to join and not ignore the rest of his group in the process.

This may seem like common sense, but you would be surprised how often guys get ignored at rush events. Rush occurs the first few weeks back from summer vacation. Brothers haven't seen each other in a few months, and are eager to catch up. The last thing they probably want to do is chat up a freshman stranger.

You have to remind them that this is the most critical two week stretch of the year. This will provide the foundation for a great year, or a mediocre one. Don't let them fall into this trap.

The fifth reason guys join fraternities is to meet girls. Some recruits think that by wearing Greek letters you instantly become a chick-magnet. Let them think this way. To win these guys over, you need to make sure you have girls at nearly all your rush events. It really doesn't matter if they are girlfriends, they need to be there. Girls can turn an average rush event into a great one.

You must remember to always treat your female guests with respect. Not only will you score points with your female guests, you will score points with the recruits. Everyone wants to be associated with true gentlemen.

The final reason is for parties. You have to be careful that the guy you are rushing is interested in more than just parties though. Believe it or not, I have heard that there are guys that join and then disappear until the night of parties. That really isn't the type of brother that makes a strong chapter. However, there is nothing wrong with a guy that enjoys parties, you just have to make sure that they are interested in the other aspects of fraternity as well.

To appeal to these guys, I would always tell them stories of great parties we had. I would explain to them that by joining a fraternity you have hundreds of people attending your party, instead of you being one of the hundreds of people who attend someone else's party. This was always an important distinction to me.

Finally, I would tell them about the road trip we organized to visit our chapter at a university six states away and the great time we had there. I would tell them about our beach party that happens every spring, and the good times that comes with it. I would back up all these stories with pictures of the events. Being able to show pictures makes the events more real for the recruit, and will have a more lasting impression. Make sure you keep pictures around to provide backup to the stories you tell.

Remember, by telling them about the past, you are giving them a glimpse into their future. You want to tell them stories about the great times you had, because they will want to have those great times as a brother in the fraternity.

Understanding the six reasons why guys join a fraternity will pay huge dividends during your next rush. You have a much better chance of getting a guy to join your fraternity if you understand what he is looking for...

Rush really can be that simple. Focus on growing your list, then focus on converting a higher number of the guys on your list into brothers.

The best part about this strategy is it minimizes effort and is easily improved semester after semester.

2 - USE YOUR CHAPTER WEBSITE TO SUPERCHARGE RECRUITMENT

It is said that about 15% of the people out there are 'always joiners'. In our case, this means that about 15% of the guys out there know that they are going to join a fraternity. Most guys end up joining the first fraternity that recruits them. Wouldn't it be great to know who those guys are so you can be the first to recruit them for your fraternity?

This chapter will detail a three step process on how you can tap into this pool of guys with minimal effort using your fraternity website and a little creativity.

Note: I am going to use the name of my school in my examples for simplicity's sake.

Step 1 - Drive These Guys to Your Chapter Website

Put yourself in a high school senior's shoes. He knows he is going to join a fraternity when he gets to college. However, he knows absolutely nothing about what fraternities are all about. So what is he going to do? He is going to google his school and fraternity to try to learn.

For example, if this kid knows he is going to attend NC State in the fall, he will google "NC State Fraternity" to learn more. He will look at the first page of google and click on the first couple of links to learn more about fraternity life.

Obviously, you want these guys coming to your chapter's site to learn more about your fraternity. That means you have to get Google to recognize your chapter for this search term.

Fortunately, that isn't too difficult to do because there is very little competition for this term.

The first thing you need to do is create a page on your chapter website with the title "NC State Fraternity". This is the page where you want all perspective recruits to go. We'll talk more about what needs to be on this page in the next step.

The key to getting this page ranked highly in Google is to get as many pages and sites as possible to link to it. It is actually a little more complicated than that, but if you focus on this point you cannot fail.

So how do you create links? First, be sure every page on your chapter website links to your "NC State Fraternity" page. Be sure all your fraternity videos link to this page (more on this in the next step). If any of the brothers have a personal website, be sure they put a link to this page on it.

A trick in the blog world is writing guest articles for other sites and using this to link to your page. The easiest way to do this is by submitting them to articles directories. Sites such as ezinearticles.com and goarticles.com allow you to publish an article on their site to include your link.

Be sure to have the chapter write a few articles and publish them on these sites, always linking back to the "NC State Fraternity" page.

Also, don't forget that you can actually pay to get your fraternity's site to show up for this term. Have your fraternity open a Google Adwords account and create an ad to drive traffic to this page. This is the lazy way to drive traffic, but could be well worth it if you get a few guys to join as result.

If you can do these few easy things, then your "NC State Fraternity" page will show up on the first page of Google, and prospective recruits will find you. This leads us to step 2:

Step 2 – Be Sure the Site is a Good Recruitment Tool

There is little value driving people to the page if it doesn't make perspective recruits want to learn more about your chapter. You can peak their interest three simple ways.

First, your "NC State Fraternity" page needs to have a lot of good pictures. Think about the things that your perspective recruit will be interested in and focus on those as subjects for pictures.

To clarify, the perspective recruits will be interested in the social scene, so be sure to have plenty of party pictures. They will be interested in girls, so be sure to have a lot of pictures with brothers hanging out with pretty girls. They will be interested in sports, so be sure to have pictures of intramural events and school games the chapter has attended. They will be curious about the chapter house, so be sure to have pictures of the house. You get the point.

An even better idea than posting pictures is to post videos. Post the best ones on Youtube and link them back to this page. Also, be sure the videos appear on the "NC State Fraternity" page as well.

Again, focus on the same ideas as in the pictures. Think about how awesome it would be to have a video of winning an intramural football game against your biggest rival on your site. Think of how impressed a potential recruit would be with video of your fraternity formal or other social events.

Another great idea is to have short interviews. Ask brothers what they get out of being a brother in the fraternity. Ask girlfriends to give a short interview. Have impromptu interviews where guests at social events are asked what makes this chapter so awesome. The more content you can deliver the better.

To maximize the goodness of these videos, create a Youtube channel and store them there. And have them all link to the "NC State Fraternity" page. This step is critical as it will build the links we talked about in Step 1.

One word of caution though - don't be stupid with the videos or pictures. Don't have booze in them. Don't have brothers who are obviously wasted. Remember to put your best foot forward, because your perspective recruits and their parents will be viewing what you post.

Finally, be sure that this page has a description of what the chapter is all about. Remember that the recruit is going to be focused on what it is in it for him. He is going to want to excel in school, but also have a good time.

Be sure the description focuses on the benefits to the potential recruit. Let him know what the big plans are for the next year. Give him examples of events that he is going to want to be a part of. This will peak his interest, and make him more likely to check your chapter out.

Step 3 – Get These Guys to Your Rush Event

At this point, you will have a page with awesome content that ranks high in Google.

However, it does you absolutely no good unless you can capture the perspective recruit's contact information.

To do that, you need to have a sign-up box on the page where the potential recruit can put his information.

However, unless there is a reason to sign-up, most people won't. You need to dangle a carrot out there to entice people to sign up.

The best idea is to offer an "NC State Welcome Packet" to those who sign up. Explain that the packet will have more information about fraternity life, but also information on how to make a successful transition from high school to college.

This should get the guys who are seriously interested to sign up to get their free packet. And when they sign up, you get their information. You have just added a high potential recruit to your names list.

The recruitment doesn't stop here though. In fact it is just starting. The Welcome Packet should contain a CD of more videos and pictures from the chapter.

It also should contain a letter from the chapter president thanking the recruit for his interest, and letting him know that if there is anything he needs that the chapter is there to help. Be sure that the letter includes an invitation to visit the chapter house whenever the potential recruit is in town. Also offer to have the brothers help him move in to his dorm room on move-in day.

In addition, it should include a sheet with the impressive Greek stats like these:

- All but two of the US presidents, since 1825 have been Greek
- There are over 9 million Greek members nationally
- 63 percent of the U.S. President's cabinet since 1900 have been Greek.
- Of the nation's 50 largest corporations, 43 are headed by fraternity men.
- 85% of the Fortune 500 executives belong to a fraternity.
- 40 of 47 U.S. Supreme Court Justices since 1910 were fraternity men.
- 76% of all Congressmen and Senators belong to a fraternity.
- Every U.S. President and Vice President, except two in each office, born since the first social fraternity was founded in 1825 have been members of a fraternity.
- A National Conference report shows a high percentage of the 4,000 NIC fraternity chapters are above the All-Men's scholastic average on their respective campuses.
- A U.S. Government study shows that over 70% of all those who join a fraternity/sorority graduate, while under 50% of all non-fraternity/sorority persons graduate.
- Less than 2% of an average college student's expenses go toward fraternity dues. (U.S. Office of Education)
- Over 85% of the student leaders on some 730 campuses are involved in the Greek community.
- 1 st Female Senator was Greek
- 1 st Female Astronaut was Greek
- All of the Apollo 11 Astronauts are Greek

- The Greek system is the largest network of volunteers in the US, with members donating over 10 million hours of volunteer service each year
- 71% of those listed in "Who's Who in America" belong to a fraternity
- As Alumni, Greeks give approximately 75% of all money donated to universities
- There are 123 fraternities and sororities with 9 million members total
- There are 750,000 undergraduate members in 12,000 chapters on more than 800 campuses in the USA and Canada

Don't forget to include tips in the packet on how to make the transition from high school to college. My suggestion is to create a report that is titled, "20 Tips to Help You Make Your Transition from High School to College". From there, just write down 20 tips that you think will help the potential recruit. Tailor it to your school to make sure it doesn't seem like a generic letter you downloaded from the internet.

At this point, you have the potential recruit's contact information. Be sure that a brother reaches out to him a week or two before class starts to see if there is anything the chapter can do to help the recruit transition to campus. Again, remind the recruit that he is always welcome to visit the chapter house.

Finally, when school begins it is time to cash in on all the hard work you have done through this project. You will have a good idea of who is serious about joining through your interactions over the summer. Be sure that everyone gets a phone call and invitation to a rush event.

Make the first rush event something simple, like a cook out at the house. This should create a non-threatening environment and entice a lot of these guys to come to the house.

From here, all that is left is to seal the deal.

While this seems like a ton of work, it will be well worth it. And actually, it will only be a ton of work the first time you do it. After that, you will only have to update information and add new pictures and videos. The hard part will have been done.

Also, after the first year you will have guys that were actually recruited using this method. It will be huge to pick their brains on how to improve this process.

Like I said earlier, 15% of the population are 'always joiners'. This is a huge chunk of the population. If you can get to them first, then chances are you will get them to join your fraternity.

3 - HOW TO CREATE AN EPIC SOCIAL PROGRAM

If you are a red-blooded, American male, you probably don't need advice on how to run your social program. I am sure you are doing just fine in that department. For that reason, I contemplated not even including this chapter in this book.

However, after a lot of thought I realize there are some younger brothers out there that could benefit from hearing my thoughts and experiences. As such, I compiled a collection thoughts that could be considered when putting together your social program.

My hope is that you will be able to incorporate some of these ideas into your social activities. I also hope that it will spur some thought and lead you into coming up with creative ideas of your own that will make your social program one of the best on campus.

Brothers Need Something to Look Forward To

If people don't have something to look forward to in life, they become depressed. People need hope and anticipation to break up the monotony of the day-to-day. Looking forward to something brings excitement to our lives, and cannot be underestimated.

Organizations are the same way. As a leader, one important goal needs to be making sure your membership is looking forward to the next great event or project. The more excitement they have in the anticipation phase, the more likely the event will be a success when it actually happens.

If you ever feel like the morale of the chapter is down, plan a social event a week or two in the future. Notice how their attitudes change when they have something to look forward to. This is the attitude you want the brotherhood to have all year.

Less is More

If you have a party every weekend, then that will become the routine. Instead of brothers looking forward to these social events, they will start to expect them.

As a result, these events will also start to lose their importance. Some brothers will justify missing an event here and there because there will always be one the next weekend. The first sign that your social program is starting to struggle is when brothers start to miss events. They won't miss events if they think each one is important.

To make each event important, have less of them and promote the heck out of the ones you do have. This will build anticipation and will make your brothers more excited about the fraternity.

There is also a huge financial benefit to having fewer social events. The money you save by having fewer events can be spent in other ways. Maybe you want to spend it on the functions you do have and make them even better. Maybe you want to make upgrades to the house. Maybe you can use this money to offset the cost of formal.

Regardless, having fewer parties will result in a stronger social program and will save you a lot of money. Both are great things for your chapter.

Time is Limited

Most schools have 16 week semesters. This makes planning a huge priority for the social committee, especially when considering that most of those 16 weeks are already taken.

Realize that most likely the first two weeks of every semester are dedicated to rush. The fraternity will probably have a campout and road trip each semester. There is initiation each semester. You also have spring break, Thanksgiving, Easter, Fall Break, Labor Day and Martin Luther King Day – weekends where students typically aren't in town. The last week of each semester is also shot because everyone will be cramming for finals.

When this is all added up, I figure you have 13 weekends a year, or less than 7 weekends a semester, to take care of one of the fraternity's top priorities – the social program.

As a result, be sure you pay attention to the calendar and give some thought to scheduling. You don't have as much time as you think.

Improve Your Social Reputation

Reputation is all about perception. Perception is about being memorable.

If you have a great party – people will remember that they had a great time. Simply remembering a good time is a far stretch from being memorable though.

You need to make sure your best party has a name and is an annual event for it to be truly memorable.

Think about it on your campus. Does a chapter at your school have an annual party that everyone knows about and looks forward to? At NC State back in the 90s, it was the Delta Sigma Phi Lawn Party.

This was the one Greek Event of the year that everyone knew about. Everyone made sure they attended, and it was an enormous success for Delta Sig. The event gave Delta Sig the reputation of having the best social program on campus. Because they had the reputation of the best social program, many thought they were the best fraternity on campus.

You need a flagship event if you want your social program to be recognized as one of the best on campus. This event needs to have a name and it needs to be memorable. Make this a reality and your social reputation will improve.

Adhere to the Base Theory

A common problem chapters have is getting a party started. Too often, brothers are away from the house when the party starts. When guests start to show up, no one is there. Since no one is there, the guests don't stick around and wait for the party to get good. A solution to this problem is the base theory.

The base theory stresses that you need to have a lot of people at the start of the party to ensure that the people who come later end up staying. If the party doesn't have a good base, most people will show up, stay ten minutes, and then go to a better party.

To ensure your party has a good base, stress to the brothers that they need to be at the house early. Bribe them with food if you have to. Spending a couple hundred bucks on pizzas is a great investment if it protects the thousands of dollars you have spent on the function.

Formal

Formal is the highlight of the chapter's social year. It should be an event that all brothers look forward to and plan their semester around. While I know you don't need much help planning the party, here are a few planning tips that I think will help.

Make sure everyone can afford to go. Spring already has one expensive trip – spring break. Because of spring break, I think most formals should be held in the fall. Also, be sure there are less expensive options for brothers who are tight on funds but still want to go. It is a chapter event, and you want to make sure everyone can attend.

If you choose an out-of-town formal, utilize your hotel or restaurant contacts during planning. If you need a band or a DJ, ask them who they recommend. They will be able to provide recommendations, and it will save you a lot of time researching the area.

Adhere to your risk management policy. It is easy to let your guard down because you are away from campus. Chapters get in trouble when they let their guard down. Don't fall into this trap.

Remember that you and your guests are representatives of your fraternity, university and Greek Life. Being reckless and destructive gives us all a bad name and will cost the chapter a lot of money. Don't help perpetuate the negative stereotypes fraternities already have.

Semi-Formal

A year-end banquet semi-formal is one of the most important events of the year. It is at this event that the chapter should recognize brothers who will be graduating. It is also a time to celebrate the chapter's accomplishments. Chapter awards should be given out, along with changing executive offices.

This is a fantastic way to finish the year. It will leave a positive image of the chapter with the brothers as they leave for summer, and should be used as a springboard for success in the fall.

Other semi-formal date functions are great ideas as well. Too often a brother will become completely consumed by his girlfriend and disappear from the chapter. A way to get this poor soul back to the chapter is by having an event that appeals to both him and his girlfriend. Also, this is a great event for brothers who don't have girlfriends, as it forces them to get the nerve to ask a girl out.

Semi-formals are great events and should be not be ignored in a healthy social program.

<u>Mixers</u>

Don't be afraid to ask the sorority to have a mixer with your chapter. Fraternity men are too often intimidated by sororities. Brothers will sit around during their fraternity meetings and complain for hours on end why they aren't having more mixers, but they will not have the gumption to actually ask the sorority to mix. Asking a sorority to have a mixer is a compliment. Don't ever be shy about asking. Here is how you go about making your mixer a success:

First, you have to meet with the sorority and figure out what you want to do. This means meeting with their president or social chair and discussing your intentions.

After you have agreed on the details, send the sorority a formal invitation inviting them to the mixer. Instead of mailing it, have someone hand-deliver it. This will be a nice touch.

Always stay classy. I know your fraternity brothers want the theme of the mixer to be a lingerie party or a bikini party. I hate to break it to you, but that isn't going to happen. It is extremely tacky to suggest this as a theme, and will definitely put-off the sorority. Always, always stay classy if you want to build a real relationship with the sorority.

Don't stress over selecting a theme. There are a many themes that will work great and will be a success. The one key to the theme of the mixer is there needs to be an active component to the event. The sisters and brothers have to do something together. You want to plan something that will promote interaction and make the event less awkward.

Clean the house. If you are having the event at the fraternity house – clean it. When you think it is clean, clean it again. Especially clean the bathrooms that your guests will be using. This is all about making a good impression and making your guests feel welcome.

Be presentable. Shower. Shave. Comb your hair. Press your shirt. Stick your chest out and be proud. You are a fraternity man, one of the most elite on campus. Act like it.

Make a T-shirt. This is a smart marketing move if done right. Make an awesome T-shirt that both the sorority sisters and fraternity brothers will want to wear. When they wear it on campus, people will see that your fraternity has a relationship with the sorority. That is a good thing.

Take and post pictures on your website. Again, you want to get as much mileage out of the mixer as possible. During your next rush, you want to show your rushees how awesome the mixer was instead of just telling them.

Also, this will encourage the sorority sisters to visit your fraternity's website and learn more about your fraternity. Of course, always stay classy when posting pictures. Be smart and respectful.

Make your requests wayyyyyyy in advance. Sorority calendars fill up fast. You will get left out in the cold unless you schedule months ahead.

Have an exit plan. You don't want to drag an event out forever. If you do, the last thought the sorority will have is that the mixer never ended and they couldn't wait to get out of there. That isn't good.

Finally, send a hand-written note thanking the sorority for the mixer after the successful event. This is a courtesy that will be appreciated.

Follow this advice and your mixer will be a success.

Philanthropy

The more fortunate have the moral responsibility to take care of the less fortunate. If you are a student in a fraternity, you are truly blessed to be where you are.

That doesn't mean that giving back shouldn't be fun though. Life is too short to force yourself to do things you don't enjoy. As such, be sure your philanthropy is part of your social program.

If you have a cause that means a lot to you, hold an event to raise money for it. Do what fraternities do best – create epic social events – and donate the proceeds to the noble cause.

You can raise money from these social events any number of ways. You can ask for donations at the door of a party. You can charge admission for an event like a poker tournament. You can charge for services like with a date auction. You can hold a raffle and donate the proceeds. You are only limited by your imagination.

To make it more fun and more social, you can invite a sorority to partner with you in supporting this cause.

Philanthropy doesn't have to be a drag that you do because you feel like you have to. It can be a great social event that can have a lasting impact on a lot of people.

Brotherhood Events

A key point about joining a fraternity is that it is a lot of fun. To make it as much fun as possible, the chapter needs to have many informal brotherhood events during the semester. A brotherhood event doesn't have to cost anything. The focus is to get as many guys from the chapter together to build camaraderie.

The options for brotherhood events are really limitless. There will be a potential brotherhood event for every university athletic event. While sitting together at the stadium is awesome, the event doesn't have to be anything more than meeting at the house to watch the game.

In fact, NFL Football Sundays make for one of the best recurring brotherhood events. The chapter should splurge for the NFL Ticket and put multiple TVs up in the chapter room each Sunday. Turning the chapter room into a sports bar is a great way to get brothers together to have a good time.

Another great brotherhood event is a poker night. The Texas Hold'em craze is huge right now, and there are games occurring all over campus. Why not make your house a place to hold a game?

Going to the movies as a group is another great brotherhood event. When the next big movie comes out, get a large group of brothers to go together.

One of the best brotherhood events is to have the chapter go to a concert together. When I was in school, Tom Petty was playing in town. The chapter rented a bus that took us all to the concert. It was a great time, and pretty simple to pull off.

Paintball is another great brotherhood event. Paintball normally stinks because you end up playing with jerks who have guns that are jacked up and it hurts like hell when you get shot. If you have enough guys though, you can have a field to yourself and have a lot of fun.

Intramurals should also become a brotherhood event. Having a sideline of supporters during a flag football game against your hated rival is a good time, and builds chapter spirit.

Again, the options for a brotherhood event are really limitless.

To make sure your chapter doesn't miss out on opportunities, be sure a brotherhood chair is appointed. Make sure it is a guy who regularly attends these types of events. When an event happens, have him send an email or text to the entire chapter stating the details.

Really, anyone can send the email out, but it is always good to make it someone's job so that detail doesn't get forgotten.

The purpose of brotherhood events is to get brothers together. The more the brotherhood hangs out, the better friends they become. The better friends they become the stronger your chapter will be.

Risk Management 101

Risk management isn't a fun topic, but it has to be a constant concern for the chapter's leadership team. I am sure you are well aware that your social program is the #1 way your chapter can get in trouble. There are several things you can do to greatly minimize your risk of getting in trouble.

First, be sure you appoint a sober, responsible brother to be 'in charge' of the party. This is the person who makes all decisions that night. The brotherhood must agree beforehand that they will support him. If he sees things are getting out of hand, he has the unquestioned ability to kick people out or shut the party down. If the cops show up, he is the one who talks to them. If the neighbors complain, he is the one that should try to calm them down. If people need a ride home, he can help coordinate. Having a sober, responsible brother fill this role is a crucial, initial risk management move.

Second, don't let anyone on the roof. Ever. It's just not worth it.

Third, hire someone to work security at the door and check IDs for the chapter. I know some of you worry that this will be a drag on the party, but I assure you it won't. This takes the door-keeping responsibilities away from a brother who will probably be too preoccupied with the party to do the job properly.

It also puts some of the liability on someone else should something go wrong. The security should have the ability to not allow someone into the party if they are too intoxicated and make other similar decisions. This is a wise investment and removes the brothers from making decisions they may not want to make.

Fourth, have the door security person put non-transferable, wristbands on people who are over 21. If it is a BYOB event, be sure security writes down what the person brought in. This is a good way to control what enters the event and is a good record to have in case something should happen.

Fifth, make sure the invite list is up-to-date. Open parties are a risk management violation at most schools. Be sure to provide an updated guest list so the door guy can determine who should and shouldn't be at the party.

Sixth, don't let people drive home drunk. Just because this is a difficult one to police doesn't mean that it should be ignored. Always be willing to call a cab for someone. It may be worth a couple hundred bucks to hire a van to drive people home after the party. It is part of your responsibility to your community that people get home safely after attending one of your functions.

Seventh, don't allow drugs on chapter property. This has to be hard rule for all brothers and guests.

Eighth, don't directly provide alcohol at events. The majority of your events should be BYOB if alcohol is present. If BYOB isn't an option, have a 3rd party provide it by charging for it and checking IDs. This puts the responsibility on someone else and helps alleviate the risk management concerns for the chapter.

Ninth, don't have glass bottles at your events. It just isn't worth the risk of someone getting cut if glass breaks.

Conclusion

I am confident you have no issues planning and having a good time. Most of us became involved in fraternities because of the social aspect of the organization. Hopefully these few tips will help you take your social program to the next level.

4 - HOW TO BECOME POPULAR WITH SORORITIES

At most schools, a sorority is comprised of over a hundred sisters. These girls are the smartest, prettiest and most social girls on campus. Obviously, a goal for a fraternity is to get in their good graces.

It amazes me how inept some fraternities are at developing these relationships. Most fraternities focus on wild mixers figuring that the drunker they can get the girls, the higher the probability that the girls will like them.

Other fraternities become comatose with intimidation at the very thought of sororities.

Fortunately, the following will help to break the code on how to become more popular with sororities. It is really much, much easier than fraternities make it out to be. Focus on three simple rules, and you will develop lasting relationships with the sororities on your campus.

First Rule – Develop Relationships as Individuals

You are going to have classes with sorority sisters. You are going to see them at events and at functions around campus. Go out of your way to be friendly with them.

I know, that isn't a particularly profound statement considering the title of this chapter. It is so important though that it needs to be said.

Making that transition to friend from casual acquaintance is a bit tricky though. If you have a class with the sorority sister, try to include her in your study group. If your fraternity is having a social function, be sure to invite her and her friends to it. If you can meet her off-campus, then your chances increase dramatically that you will be able to turn this acquaintance into a friend.

The benefits of these friendships are huge for the fraternity. The foundation for relationships between chapters is relationships between people. If you can develop friendships with the sorority sisters, it won't take long before you will have a relationship with the sorority.

Rule Two – Develop Relationships as Organizations

While being social to develop individual relationships is important, the real goal is to develop relationships between chapters. You do that by focusing on giving as much as you can to the sorority, while expecting nothing in return.

This is a tough concept for a lot of people to understand. We live in the 'what can you do for me' society, so this is a foreign concept to a lot of people.

Unfortunately, most people are only concerned with what is in it for them. If you can change your fraternity's thought process from the taker mindset to the giver mindset you will be amazed at how eager the sorority will be to develop a relationship with your fraternity.

To start giving to the sorority, here is what you do... Have the fraternity president meet with someone on the sorority's leadership team (preferably the president). Let her know that the fraternity is interested in developing a relationship with the sorority.

Offer to help them with the sorority's philanthropy. The sorority will have events to raise money or awareness for causes important to them. Simply offer to help in any way you can.

There is not a sorority in the country that will turn down an offer like that. Some of the events they put on are pretty involved, and they need all the hands they can get to help out.

Some great things will happen as a result from the fraternity giving their time to help the sorority.

First, the sorority will realize that the guys in the fraternity are pretty decent because of the genuineness of their assistance.

Second, the sisters will get to work with the brothers on these events which will help to develop those individual relationships. Finally, both organizations will be making contributions to a good cause everyone wins when that happens.

If the sorority is inclined, offer to host a joint philanthropy with the sorority. If they are particularly passionate about an issue, let the philanthropy benefit their cause. Again, this will give both organizations the opportunity to get to know each other better and relationships will develop from those experiences.

If the opportunity presents itself, don't hesitate to try to get some positive publicity for the sorority for what they is doing. The amount of negative press directed at Greek Organizations is overwhelming, and we should never let an opportunity pass to get positive recognition for members of our Greek Community.

Again, be sure that it is all about the sorority. Your goal is to make them look good. Let the school paper and local paper know about the event. Make a couple quick calls to the local news stations. Publicize the event on each brother's Facebook pages. Everyone likes to be recognized for doing a good deed, so make sure the sorority gets the recognition they deserve.

At the conclusion of the event, be sure to thank the sorority. Sure, they should probably be thanking you, but remember it isn't about you, it is about them. Send them a note thanking them for letting you be a part of their event.

Working jointly on a philanthropy is the surest, safest place to start. After that, you can discuss the potential of more social ideas.

Another great idea is to have a joint new member event. There are literally thousands of ideas that would make for an awesome joint new member night. The obvious benefit here is that the youngest members of both organizations will develop friendships that could benefit both chapters for the next four years.

Finally, be sure to invite them to your social events. If you want a sorority to attend your event, it probably makes sense to take the time to invite them.

Send a short, hand-written invitation to the sorority and invite them to attend. I can assure you with almost 100% certainty that the sorority will send at least a few girls to the event because that is the polite thing to do when you are invited. Sorority sisters pride themselves on etiquette, and they will be sure their organization makes an appearance.

When the sisters show up, be sure to greet them and follow the rules below about being a gentleman. Also, be sure to follow-up and send a thank you note letting them know how much you appreciate them attending your function.

Rule Three – Always Be a Gentleman

You will not succeed in developing relationships with sororities or sorority sisters if you are not a gentleman. While the following isn't an all-encompassing list, it is a good set of rules for every fraternity gentleman. Always be mindful how you and your brothers conduct yourselves. This will become your reputation, and thus will become the reputation of your chapter.

1) Don't swear – When in the presence of ladies, don't toss F bombs around like you are in the locker room. The type of girls you should be interested in aren't interested in your salty language.

2) Look presentable – Iron your pants and shirt. Shave. Comb your hair. You don't have to look like you just got out of a GQ magazine, but you should look like you give a damn.

3) Stand up when a woman enters the room or gets up from a table. This is a common courtesy that has been lost on this generation.

4) Stand up straight – Don't slouch. Stand tall and stick out your chest. Have confidence and be proud of who you are.

5) Talk about them, not yourself – If you want a woman to become interested in you, be interested in them. Ask questions and find out what they like. By letting them talk, they will think that you are a

great conversationalist, even though all you did was listen and ask questions.

6) Don't be late – It is rude to leave a woman waiting. Be considerate with their time.

7) Brush your teeth – The quickest way to leave a bad impression is by having bad breath. Brush your teeth and gargle mouthwash before you meet a woman.

8) Don't chew gum – People who chew gum look like cows smacking their cud. Don't be this guy.

9) Don't interrupt – If you walk up on a conversation, politely listen and look for an opportune time to join in. If someone is telling a story, politely wait for them to finish before speaking.

10) Remove your hat indoors – Again, another courtesy lost on this generation. Hats are for outside, not inside. You don't play for the Yankees, so take your hat off.

11) Open doors – Opening doors is an age-old courtesy that never loses it's importance. It is a shockingly simple sign of respect.

12) Ask if she needs anything – It is always polite to ask someone if there is anything you can get for them to make their visit more enjoyable.

13) Maintain eye contact – Having wandering eyes during conversations is a sign that you are not really interested in what the person is saying. Fight the urge to scan the room by focusing on the person you are having the conversation with.

14) Remember names – Do everything you can to remember the names of the person you have just met. Use their name

immediately after they tell it to you. Try to associate the name with something you will remember. Remembering a person's name is one of the simplest things you can do to show someone you care about them.

15) Introduce others – If someone walks up to a conversation, introduce the person to your guest if there is even the slightest doubt that they may not know their name. This saves a lot of awkward embarrassment for all involved.

16) Make small talk – The key to making small talk is very simple. You need to ask open-ended questions. The most common conversation starter in college is asking what is your major? This question isn't good because the person you are talking to will give you a one-word answer. Ask open-ended questions that forces the person to give you some information about them. This gives you the opportunity to ask more questions and have an interesting conversation.

17) Don't answer your phone – Leave your phone in your pocket. Don't answer calls. Doing so shows that the call is more important than the person you are talking to. The same rule goes for texts.

18) Give compliments, but don't overdue it – People like to hear nice things about them. Be sure to toss a compliment or two into the conversation, but don't overdue it...

19) Always follow up with a thank you note – If someone does anything for you, take the time to say thank you. This is a common courtesy that goes a long way with people.

20) Don't forget the small details – The small details are very important. It shows you are genuine, and it shows you care. Be sure to send a card to the sorority for their founder's day and the

sorority's birthday. These simple gestures will let the sorority know that you care about the relationship, and they will return the favor.

Sororities don't have to be intimidating. If you focus on trying to make friends by doing the things friends typically do for each other, you will be able to form meaningful relationships.

The hardest part is being willing to initiate the conversation and getting over that initial awkwardness. However, if you have the courage to do so, it will be one of the best moves you could ever make for your fraternity.

5 – THE RIGHT WAY TO RUN A NEW MEMBER PROGRAM

This chapter is designed to give you ideas that will help you create a challenging new member program that will turn your new members into productive, contributing brothers.

Remember that the most important trait of a new member program is it has to be fun. If it isn't fun, then the brothers will not be involved, and the new members will learn to dread the fraternity. You can't let that happen.

Be creative and teach the new members how to love the fraternity. If you can do that, then your new member program will be a success.

New Member Program

The foundation of a new member program should be the new member task board. This should be a list of tasks the new member class will have to accomplish before they are initiated. The brotherhood should have a meeting before the new member period starts to determine if there are any tasks that need to be added to the list. This ensures everyone is involved in this process.

The task board should be only shown to brothers and new members. Outsiders should not be able or welcome to see the board.

Having a task board will give the new member class a very clear objective for becoming a brother. This clear goal will motivate the new members, and will push them to achieve more.

A typical task board should include some variation of the following examples:

Task 1: Attend all New Member Nights

Each new member nights will be scheduled before the start of the new member program, so there should be no excuse for missing one. The following are examples of potential new member nights:

New Member Photo Album Hunt

This purpose of this event is to build camaraderie in the new member class. Chances are that the new members really don't know each other this early in their new member period. This event will serve as a fun 'icebreaker' for the class.

The event will start with the new member educator giving the new member class a list of photos that they will need to take.

At the end of the night, the new member class should have a collection of fun pictures and a lot of good stories to tell. The new members will take their pictures and put them in an album. This should instill a sense of belonging for the young new member class.

As always, be sure the photos are in good taste.

Sorority Serenade

The purpose of this event is to introduce the new member class to sorority life.

This event will start with a challenge. The challenge for the new member class is they have to get a T-shirt from every sorority on campus, and at least one for every new member.

To do this, the new members have to serenade each sorority at your school.

The new members must remember to let the sorority know of their upcoming new member party. They should present the sisters with a formal invitation to the event. They should tell the sisters that the new member will wear the shirt they just received to the party if they promise to show up. It would be an awesome sight to see every new member wearing a shirt from a different sorority at the party.

This event will be a ton of fun for the new member class. Making sure the new members fall in love with the fraternity is a key priority for the first few weeks of the new member period. This event will help achieve that goal.

New Member Party

The purpose of this event is to see what type of energy and creativity the new member class possesses.

Teaching the new members how to throw a party is an important part of their development.

The new member class will have a budget for the party, and little other guidance. They are to request any assistance they need from the brothers, and the brothers will give it without trying to take over the event. Are the new members going to make mistakes? Of course they will. However, they will learn from these mistakes and become better brothers for it.

Campout

Fraternity campouts normally turn into drinking in the woods. While that is a lot of fun, it really doesn't do much to develop brotherhood. It does develop drinking buddies, but not a new member class.

For this campout, the setting is in a state forest. I would chart out a hike that the new members have to accomplish on their own. They would start off on the hike in the morning, and hike till the middle of the afternoon. At the end of their hike, they would meet the rest of the chapter who will have the camp site chosen, and everything set up.

The hike gives the new members the opportunity to bond and a chance to accomplish something together. A hike isn't an easy task for everyone, and will seem like a major achievement to some. Most importantly though, it gives the new members time to bond and become closer friends.

Their reward at the end of their task would be a campout feast prepared for them by the brotherhood.

After the feast, there will be a few tasks the new members have to accomplish.

First, the each new member will have to stand up in front of the brotherhood and roast or toast his big brother (new member's choice). It is important that the new members know their big brothers well by this stage of the new member period - well enough to be able to give a speech about them. The new members will know that they are going to have to give this talk, and they will know of this requirement early in the new member period.

Second, there needs to be some type of competition at campout. As juvenile as it sounds, it is a hell of a lot of fun to play capture the flag in the woods at night. Make sure you do something like that, and make sure everyone in the fraternity can participate.

A well-planned camp out will give the new member class a sense of accomplishment. Having the entire chapter recognize their achievement will do wonders for the morale of the new member class. This is the perfect goal for the middle of the new member period.

Road Trip to Another Chapter

One of the best parts about being in a fraternity is that the organization is bigger than just one chapter at one school. It is important to teach a new member class this, and the best way to do that is to have them take a road trip.

That being said, it probably isn't a good idea to send a new member class to another chapter alone. There will always be the fear that the chapter you send them to will decide to haze your new members the entire weekend. This is the last thing you want. Therefore, it is a good idea to send a few brothers (or many if they want to go) with them to ensure the new members are treated properly.

For the destination, pick a school that is close to yours to make transportation easy. Make sure that the new members always ride together and eat together. This is a quick and easy way to help them forge strong relationships.

Then, show them the best time of their life at the other school.

Encourage the new members to talk to the brothers and new members of the other chapter to see if they can learn anything from them. Every chapter does things a little different, and it would be great to be able to borrow an idea that could be used to strengthen your own chapter.

This event is designed to be fun for the brothers and the new members. A road trip is one of those things that is pretty hard to screw up. More times than not, a road trip will be the highlight of the new member period.

Brotherhood Dinner

After a few new member events, the new members should have a good idea of what the fraternity is all about. They should have had a great time, and they will probably be pretty gung-ho about the fraternity.

This is the perfect time to bring them back to earth and have them reflect on what they have learned. To do that, tell the new member class that they are to prepare a dinner for the brotherhood. Let them know that the dinner will be for brothers and new members only, and everyone will be in shirt and tie. Impress upon the new member class that they are to put their best foot forward to impress the brotherhood.

After the dinner is prepared, and the meal is eaten together. Have *the brothers* clear the tables after the meal. Then, have the new members tell the brotherhood what the fraternity means to them. They won't be given a warning this time about having to get up and talk. You don't want their answers to be scripted. You want their answers to come from the heart.

If the brotherhood has done their job to this point, then the new members will be gushing about how great the fraternity is and how excited they are to become brothers. This will be a good indicator for the brothers of the strength of the new member program. It will also be a good indicator about the health of the fraternity.

After the new members speak, allow the brothers to join in as well. It is important to reflect and appreciate how awesome it is to be a brother in a fraternity. Teach the new members to do this early, and you will have a stronger brotherhood.

New Member Movie Night

A key to a new member period is to get the new member class to work on as many things together as possible. Each time they accomplish a task together, they become closer. A great way to do that is to have them make a movie together.

To set up the event, let the new members know that on this night in the new member period they are going to premier their movie for the brotherhood. They have the previous seven weeks to make the movie.

Let them figure out all the details of the movie. Also, let them know they are to keep the content secret from the brothers so it will be a surprise for all when it is played for the first time.

At worst, the brotherhood will have a good laugh because the movie is so terrible that you can't help but laugh. At best, the movie will be a riot. Either way, the brotherhood and the new member class will have a good time watching it. The real benefit will be the hours the new member class spent together to produce something for the brotherhood.

New Member Rush Event

It amazes me how a fraternity will spend months teaching a new member class about the brotherhood, but won't spend any time educating the class on rush. Recruitment is the single most critical skill a fraternity must possess, otherwise it will fold.

It is imperative that the new member period spends a little time educating the new member class on how to recruit. There is no better way to learn than to learn by doing. So it makes sense to have the new members actually host a rush event.

First though, don't send them out blind. Have the couple brothers who are the best recruiters sit down and teach the new members what they know about fraternity recruitment. Make the new members read the recruitment advice on thefraternityadvisor.com. There are over 100 pages dedicated to high quality, fraternity recruitment education on the site.

Once the new members have some clue as to what they are doing, have them set up a rush event. They have to plan the event, to include finding guys to come out. Obviously, this is really a rush event for the entire chapter, even though it is led by the new member class. Give the new member class a goal of how many guys they need to bring out, and make sure the brothers help the new members achieve that goal.

An essential, but often forgotten part of fraternity recruitment is keeping contact information of the guys who come out for the event. Make sure the new member class knows to keep good records so they can follow up with the guys they brought out.

Again, this is an event that can be nothing but positive for the chapter and the new member class. Rush events are supposed to be fun (if they aren't fun it is a pretty terrible recruitment event), so everyone should have a good time. Also, it should give the chapter a jumpstart on the next semester's rush. Most importantly, it should give the soon-to-be brothers an introduction into rush before they are thrown into the fire the next semester.

Task 2: Signatures

Each new member should get 3 signatures from each brother. This one is quite simple. If a new member is joining a fraternity, he must know every brother. This is a way to make sure there are at least three interactions between every brother and new member during the semester. The three signatures are symbolic, and they should represent the following:

The first signature should be given by the brother when the new member asks for it. Nothing more, nothing less.

The second signature should be given at the conclusion of a new member/brother interview. That does mean that each new member will have to interview every brother.

The final signature should be after the brother and new member do something together. It can be as simple as having dinner together, or hanging out at the house one night. The goal is not to haze the new member, but to make sure that the new members know every brother before they join the fraternity.

Task 3: House Improvement Project

The new member class should complete a house improvement project. The new member class needs to learn of the importance of the chapter house and giving back to the fraternity. Creating a house improvement project is a great way to instill this mindset.

Let the new members pick their project. Make sure they work on it together, and that it benefits the house. They can build a bar, build benches, paint rooms, clear out the backyard, plant bushes – whatever they think will be a great addition to the house.

If every class has this type of project, every class will have an appreciation and take pride in the house because they will have had a part in making it what it is today.

Task 4: New Member Exam

Pass a new member exam. Every fraternity has a manual of information that the new members must learn before they become brothers. Often, this involves memorizing creeds and other important fraternity information.

To ensure the new members actually take the time to learn the material, they need to be tested on it. The test needs to be administered once a week. If everyone in the class passes the test, then the class no longer has to take the test and this task will be considered complete. However, if one person fails, then the entire class fails for the week.

In addition, the test will be given to the new members in advance. Nothing is more frustrating than being 'tricked' when being tested on material. If the intent is to make sure the new members know the material. Let them know what is expected of them, and let them accomplish this task.

Task 5: Talk with Executive Director

Have a discussion with the executive director of the fraternity. The executive director is an intimidating person in the eyes of most brothers. He is seen as the evil guy from nationals that is only out to screw you and the chapter. That couldn't be further from the truth.

The executive director is a guy who believes in the fraternity so much that he decided to make it his career. He has decided to give back to the fraternity that gave so much to him. You can learn a lot from a man like this.

This task requires the new member class to schedule a conference call with the executive director. They need to email him, and schedule a time for a one hour conversation. All the new members need to be present and part of the conversation.

The new members should be prepared with questions for the executive director. Really, they should ask anything. The executive director is a wealth of knowledge about the fraternity on a much larger scale than just one chapter. He will be able to give the new member class a perspective that the brotherhood doesn't have.

There are a couple benefits to this task. The new members will learn more about the fraternity from the conversation. Also, they will meet a valuable resource who could help them and the chapter later in their college career. Finally, the executive director learns more about the chapter, and will be more apt to help if needed because a relationship will be established.

Task 6: Talk with an Alum

Have a discussion with an alumnus from the chapter. While the conversation with the executive director is a group task, the discussion with an alumnus from your chapter is an individual task.

Each new member needs to have a talk with at least one alumnus during the semester. Hopefully, the alumni chair is good enough where he can advise which alumni the new members should meet. If he isn't, the new members can be on their own to find an alum to meet.

The goal is simple. A new member will get to meet a brother who has finished their college career, and will be able to listen to the positive impacts that fraternity had on him. He will also make a valuable contact that might be able to help him later on.

Task 7: New Member Paddle

My first memory from my first visit to a fraternity house was seeing the fraternity paddles hanging over the fireplace. That was a vivid memory for me, and it definitely added to the aura surrounding the fraternity.

New member paddles are a tradition that is important. However, like a lot of things in life, it can be cheapened. The new members should be required to make their paddles out of a block of wood. This will give them a sense of satisfaction when complete, and it will give meaning to the process. Once it is complete, it should be displayed proudly at the chapter house.

Also, it isn't cool to ever hit anyone with a paddle. Anyone who has ever been hit with one knows that it really hurts. There really is not room for that in a civilized society.

Task 8: Big and Little Brother Dinner

Big Brothers and Little Brothers should have dinner together. The big brother/little brother relationship is an important one in the fraternity. To make sure the big brother and little brother get off on the right foot, the big brother should take the little brother to dinner – big brother's treat.

The meal doesn't have to be anything fancy, but it has to be just the two of them. Hopefully the big brother will be serious about his commitment to his little brother, and serve as the mentor the little brother needs during his new member program and into brotherhood.

Task 9: New Member GPA

Show the new member educator every graded piece of class work. If your fraternity's new members flunk out of school, then all the time and energy the brotherhood spent on them will be wasted.

Most new members are freshman, and most freshmen have bad study habits. They are out on their own for the first time, and probably are unprepared for the rigors of college life.

The fraternity has to be their brother's keeper and make sure the new members get through their new member period with decent grades. As a side benefit, the university will track the new member GPA, and will penalize the chapter if the new members do poorly. Don't let this happen.

At the start of the new member program, the new member educator needs to receive a copy of every syllabus from every class from every new member. Then, he needs to make a giant calendar that shows the dates of each graded assignment. This calendar is for the brotherhood only – the new member class and outsiders do not need to see it or even know about it.

The new member will then be required to show the educator every graded assignment from the semester, and the grade will be posted on the calendar. This is not done to ridicule the new members, and the new members will not know this is done until they become brothers. The reason for this is so the brotherhood can remain informed about the academic standing of the new members. If a new member bombs a calculus class, the brotherhood will know it because they will be able to see it on the calendar.

When this happens the educator will be able to investigate why the new member failed the assignment. If it was because he was lazy, he is there to give the new member a kick in the pants. If it is because he didn't understand the material, the brothers who are strong in this area can assist the new member with his studies. The best part is the educator will know about the problem, so the fraternity can help the new members that need help.

The calendar also provides another benefit. Most freshmen will be taking introductory classes and will be taking the associated standardized tests on the same day. If the brotherhood is aware of this, they can set up study sessions to assist the new members with their preparation.

For example, at my school nearly every freshman took chemistry as a freshman. Chemistry tests were standardized across the school. The night before the test, a senior who majored in Chemistry would get the new member class together for a last minute review session. This was huge for the class, and they learned more in that few hours than probably the entire semester. The new members got better grades because the brothers were aware of their test and took the time to help the new members prepare.

There is also the benefit that the new members will probably be more focused on their studies because they know the fraternity will be checking up on them. Pride will encourage most new members to get good grades because the last thing they want is for someone to know they didn't do well in class.

Nothing but good came come of this program. The new members will get off to a great start to their college career, and an environment where academics are important will be created (if it already doesn't exist). The new member GPA will become something that the entire chapter will be proud of.

Task 10: Fundraise Dues

The new member class should not have to pay dues. I know that this is a crazy notion for cash-strapped fraternities out there. There are huge benefits to this idea though, and the new members will end up paying for their recruitment anyway by fundraising through this task.

First, imagine the impact this would have for the fraternity during recruitment. It will allow the fraternity to be more selective during rush, while increasing the size of new member classes.

At the start of the new member period, the new members should be given access to the new member class checking account. However, to ensure nothing screwy happens, make sure all checks and withdrawals need to be co-signed by the new member treasurer *and* the new member educator.

The new members will have to pay certain bills to the brotherhood out of this account. These bills should be clearly established. For example, they will need to pay for their new member dues to nationals and to the university.

With the rest of money in the account, they need to accomplish the tasks on the task board and whatever other stuff they need for their new member period. This will teach them fiscal responsibility which is important in any organization.

This task though will be for them to leave the next new member class with more money than this class started with. To do this, they will obviously need to fund-raise during the semester. Fortunately, motivated new members can put on great fundraising events. Be sure they read the chapter on How to Fundraise $40,000. The new member class needs to tap into these ideas and come up with their own to build the account.

That being said, the last thing the chapter wants is to make the new members fund-raise in the wrong way. All events should be fun. If they aren't fun, then don't do them!

It is better for the new member class to fail in filling up the account than have them quit because they are sick of doing miserable fundraising gigs. Don't ever let fraternity be a drag. It is very possible to have a great time, and make a lot of money too.

Hell Week & Initiation:

The final steps of the new member program for most chapters is hell week and initiation.

There should not be a hell week in any new member program. The traditional fraternity hell week is a juvenile concept that has no room in a fraternity that is designed to build men.

Once the new members have completed their tasks, it should be time to initiate them into the brotherhood.

This should be done in strict accordance to the ritual. All hazing should be removed from this experience. Hazing during the most sacred rights of passage in the fraternity makes a mockery of the very ideals that are the foundation of the fraternity. Don't cheapen the experience of an event that should be a celebration for both the new members and the brothers.

At the conclusion of initiation, the chapter should throw a huge initiation party. If there is ever a cause for celebration, it is when the brotherhood welcomes new members into the organization.

Welcome them into the brotherhood the right way, with a night they'll remember.

I think you will agree that cumulatively this sample collection of tasks will be pretty challenging to accomplish in a single semester. Pushing your new member class in a productive way will ensure that you are only initiating the most dedicated and highest quality men.

I also hope you see that these events and tasks will be a ton of fun for all involved, and will accomplish the goal of the program – turning new members into good brothers.

Make your program fun and challenging. Avoid hazing. This is how you turn naïve freshman into solid, contributing brothers.

6 – HOW TO MAKE FINANCE A CHAPTER STRENGTH

Fraternity finance is not a sexy topic, and often the treasurer is not a popular guy because of his responsibility to collect dues.

This is extremely unfortunate for most chapters. The financial program is probably the single most important program to develop leadership in the brotherhood. If done right, it can also make brothers more engaged than you ever thought possible.

Remember that as you go through this chapter. If you can master this area of your fraternity, then your chapter will achieve fantastic things.

Collecting Dues

Getting brothers to pay their dues gives some chapters countless headaches. This isn't earth-shattering or exciting, but I will include it in this chapter for the sake of completeness.

Getting brothers to pay their dues is a simple formula. First, brothers must realize the financial commitment they are making, and agree to it every semester by signing a brotherhood contract.

The contract needs to be detailed enough to explain the consequences for not paying their dues on time.

Then, it is the entire chapter's responsibility to ensure that each brother is held accountable for meeting their obligation. To do that, the treasurer must include the names of every brother who owes dues in his financial report during chapter meetings. The rest of the chapter needs to create an environment where being delinquent isn't acceptable, and you do that by making it uncomfortable to be late on your dues.

While this may seem like a jerk move, you are actually doing the delinquent brother a huge favor. If the brother neglects his obligations to his closest friends (his brothers) then think about what is going to happen when he has a family to support.

Is he going to neglect to pay his mortgage because he doesn't feel like it? Is he going to neglect to make his car payment because something else strikes his fancy? By teaching him to be responsible at this stage in life, you are helping instill the values necessary for him to become a responsible member of society.

There are going to be times though that this doesn't work. When that happens, you need to take the brother to small claims court. The process is quite simple. Just fill the paperwork out at your local courthouse and explain the case to the judge on your court date. If you have your brotherhood contract in hand, this will be an open and shut case.

Again, I realize some of you will feel this is harsh. However, you must remember that these delinquent brothers are stealing from the rest of the chapter. The chapter still has to pay dues to nationals and the IFC for the delinquent brother. He is probably still participating in social functions. If he isn't contributing by paying his dues, he is freeloading off the chapter.

There is another benefit to doing this. By taking a brother to small claims court, you are sending a very strong message to the brotherhood. This will ensure they take their responsibilities seriously, because they will not want to be in the same position. This is a very powerful deterrent.

That's it. That is all you need to do to ensure you get 100% of the brothers to pay their dues. Brothers have to know that they are going to be held accountable for their obligations. That is a staple in every world class organization.

However, if you stop here, you really aren't making your chapter better, you are just meeting basic expectations.

Fraternity Finance is the Truest Reflection of the Strength of a Fraternity

When you hold a leadership position in your chapter, you are making a commitment to your brothers. You are telling them that you are going to do everything in your power to ensure that the fraternity is meeting their expectations. But what does that mean?

Every brother has basic expectations of what they are to receive by being a brother. While you have probably never thought about it this way, fraternity dues are basically a value proposition. Essentially, all of us had to determine if the money we pay in dues is worth what we receive in return.

An average leader will probably not realize this is part of their job, and they'll strive to do whatever has been done in the past and hope the brothers remain happy. The brothers won't know any better, so they will continue paying their dues because they are getting the same value they always received.

However, a great leader will realize there is power in giving more than expected. This is a very valuable lesson, and is true in any organization and in any position. *If you want to be a great leader, you must consistently strive to exceed expectations.*

A great leader will look to provide as much value as possible with the dues collected. Then, the great leader will look to create even more value though fundraising. Let me give you an example.

Let's say the brothers have a basic expectation of having two social events per semester and one formal. For simplicity's sake, let's say that is all they want, and that is all they have ever received.

An average leader would give the brothers exactly what they expect. They would have the two social events and one formal, and it would probably be a mirror image of the ones last year.

A great leader will look to give more. Maybe he will have three parties in addition to the formal. Maybe he'll incorporate new events, which the brothers won't expect but will be really eager to have. Maybe he will incorporate new ideas into the old events, which will knock the socks off of the brothers.

In this situation, the brothers will realize they are getting tremendous value for their dues, and they will be more eager to pay.

Let me give an example:

My chapter rented a bus to go on a road trip to the University of Illinois. Realize that NC State is a hell of a long way from Illinois.

This idea was one the brothers never dreamed of, but it was exactly the type of value that made them appreciate their membership.

As a result of this trip, the brothers understood they were getting great value for their dues and collecting dues became much easier. (I will discuss more about this trip in a later chapter.)

Exceeding expectations is a great way to measure the morale and strength of the chapter. If the brothers are eager to pay their dues because they think they are getting tremendous value for their money, then the leadership team is doing a good job.

Again, I can't overstate the importance of this concept. Great leaders become that way by exceeding expectations. If your chapter does that then it will reflect in your dues collection. Brothers will not want to miss out on the tremendous value the fraternity provides.

Use Fraternity Finance to Develop Leadership in Your Brothers

Getting the leadership team to exceed expectations is huge, and the brotherhood will respond favorably to this. However, you can take it a step further, and achieve even greater results.

You do that by empowering the brotherhood to be in control of the chapter's finances.

Each committee should be given a budget. They should have the freedom to spend this money as they see fit to benefit the chapter.

Obviously the leadership team needs to have a part in guiding each committee to ensure that the money is spent in a responsible manner, but you want the ultimate responsibility to rest with the committee.

From there, the leadership team needs to coach the committee chairs to exceed expectations in their positions. Their budgets are a valuable tool needed to achieve that goal.

If you can do that, you can count on four major accomplishments:

First, by empowering the brothers, you are making them as engaged as possible in the chapter. They will be ultimately responsible for the chapter's success or failure, and this responsibility is something that the brotherhood craves.

Second, you will be teaching your brothers how to manage a budget for the benefit of the fraternity. You will show them how leaders focus on exceeding expectations. This is developing leadership in your chapter.

Third, by making the brotherhood directly responsible for their budgets, they will understand where the fraternity's finances are spent. They will realize the importance of timely payments, and will be motivated to ensure that all brothers pay on time.

Finally, the leadership team will learn a valuable skill, the ability to delegate authority. This leverages the talents of the leadership team allowing them to accomplish more than ever before. This is another skill that separates average leaders from great ones.

House Finance

The house can be a fraternity's biggest asset or liability. A fraternity house that drains the bank account each semester will eventually destroy the chapter.

It is absolutely essential that the house be a self-sustaining entity financially. By that, I mean that chapter funds should never be needed to make ends meet when paying the rent/mortgage.

The way to do that is simple on paper, tough in real life. The chapter will know what the rent/mortgage is, and they know how much the bills will be (approximately). This is the total amount of cash the fraternity needs to bring in to make the house a viable option.

Most chapters then figure out how many brothers will live in the house, divide number by the total owed, and that is the rent. And that is a recipe for disaster.

It will spell disaster because all rooms aren't created equal. How do you charge a brother in a huge room with its own bathroom the same price as guys that have to double up in bedroom that really is a converted closet? How do you know you are providing a fair value for the brothers? If you don't know the answers to these questions, the conversation about who is going to live in the house next year will be painful.

The solution to this problem can be accomplished many ways. The best way is for the house committee to set a price for each room in the house. The price should be set comparable to the equivalent prices around campus.

Then, let the brothers select their rooms. If the brother lived in that room the previous year, they will have the first right on it. If not, the older brother gets the rights. This should eliminate fights over rooms.

Hopefully the prices are set so the house can turn a profit for the chapter. This should be the goal. If you can't make that happen, everything will be great as long as the cash-in equals the cash-out.

One strange thing may happen in this situation. Some brothers may choose to room together in order to live cheaply. This is a great thing. The more brothers that the chapter can get to live in the house - the better.

Another thing to remember is all leases must be 12 months. My chapter got in big financial trouble one year because we let our brothers have 10 month leases. We assumed we would be able to fill the house with other brothers over the summer. We were wrong, and it crippled us financially.

Be sure to do everything possible to make the house appealing to brothers. If the house has parking near campus, that could be a big draw. Splurge and get all the Directv packages. Of course, make sure these perks can fit into the budget.

Make the house a desirable place to live in, and it could become a solid, money-making asset for the chapter.

One side note – the brothers who do not live in the house should have to pay nominally higher dues for not living in the house. It doesn't have to be more than $50 a semester.

This will make the house a more attractive option for brothers financially. It will make the brothers who live in the house feel more appreciated. It will make the brothers who don't live in the house able to show that they are contributing. It is really a win-win for all.

Use these tips to not only make finance a strength in your chapter, but also a tool to develop leadership in your brotherhood.

Don't ever forget that your job as a leader is to provide as much value to the chapter as possible. If you strive to do that, you cannot fail.

7 – HOW TO RAISE $40,000 FOR YOUR CHAPTER

Fundraising is a critical piece of fraternity finance. A few successful fundraising events will have a profound impact on your chapter finances.

This is a list of 18 easy fundraising ideas which you can implement in your chapter. Of course, you can't do all 18, but you can select a few which you think your chapter can pull off. The figures I used are based on a 50 man chapter. In my estimation this is the average chapter size.

There are a couple of things you need to remember with fundraising. First, the event has a higher probability of being successful when they are fun. Next, publicizing your event in most cases is 95% of the work. Finally, don't forget to up-sell when possible.

Best of luck on your fundraising projects.

Fraternity Poker Tournament

Potential Profit: $2500+

Planning Required: High

Partner Recommended: Yes

Chances are, your fraternity already has a weekly poker night. If you don't, you need to start one because it is a great way for brothers to spend time together.

You can also host a poker night as a fundraiser for your fraternity. This event has big potential if you are motivated enough to put the effort into making it a quality event.

First off, you want to partner with a sorority. Split the profits with them 50/50. They will bring a lot of value to this relationship.

Sororities are normally a lot more organized than fraternities and that will help with planning. Also, remember your target audience is 95% guys. They will be more eager to participate if the event is sponsored by a sorority.

You will need to reserve a large enough room to hold the event. Remember that you want to keep costs to a minimum, so try to find a free place.

Have the brothers be dealers if they aren't playing, and hire a third party to serve drinks. Be sure you work out a deal where you split part of their profits.

Have the sisters around to take care of all the odds and ends of the event (registration, prizes, passing out chips, ect).

Place the entry fee at $25 (or more). This fee will entitle each player to $1000 in chips. Also, allow players to rebuy in the tournament the first hour. This will encourage players to purchase an additional $1000 in chips for $25, because they will be at a severe disadvantage if they don't.

Make an agreement with the sorority that each organization will find at least 100 people to enter the tournament. Make sure that both organizations are tapping into all their networks when you advertise the event. You should be able to find 200 fraternity guys who want to sign up. Don't forget to use all your networks to publicize the event.

If you get 200 players, and assume half rebuy, then you will have raised $7500. Spend $2500 on prizes, and give each organization $2500. This is a very conservative estimate of the potential profits of this event.

Remember that gambling isn't looked at too highly in university circles. You probably should not give cash out as a prize. You should give prizes though. Be sure that both the sorority and fraternity are trying to solicit donations for prizes. At the very least, attempt to get discounts on stuff to buy as prizes.

Make sure the top 20% of the players are awarded prizes. The top ten or so should be good prizes, with the top prize obviously being very good.

Don't forget there are other ways to make a profit off the event as well. Sell T-shirts promoting the event. Have a silent auction in the middle of the event. Be sure to maximize your potential profit!

If the event is done well, then this is one that could be repeated every semester. Don't forget that you will have formed a successful partnership with the sorority which could have an even more significant impact on your fraternity than the financial benefit.

Ask the University for Funding

Potential Profit: $1000+

Planning Required: Medium

Partner Recommended: Yes and No

There are organizations on your campus that have money, and they want you and other student organizations to spend it.

I know this is hard to believe. After all, fraternities spend most of their time worrying about who is out to get them. There are powerful groups out there that can help you.

The biggest of which is student government. Each university's student government has a significant budget that they can allocate however they wish. Also, university housing has money. So does the alumni group, IFC and the chancellors office. The beauty is, all these organizations have a budget and are obligated to promote causes that will benefit the student body.

The key to receiving this funding is to make sure you have a legitimate request in the eyes of those organizations. While a beach party is always a great idea, it will be hard for those organizations to justify giving you money to help support it.

My fraternity held an annual scholarship given to the student who best exemplified eliminating prejudice. Every student on campus was eligible for the scholarship, except for the brothers in our chapter.

When it was time to hold a banquet to announce the winner, we went to the university alumni group for help. They gladly paid for the banquet room and refreshments for our presentation ceremony because they believed in the cause.

Another group on our campus would go to the student government every year to receive funding to host a huge concert. The money raised from this concert went to a very worth-while charity which the student government was proud to support. Every other fraternity on campus was upset that this fraternity would receive the funding every year, but they were too lazy to ask for funding for their initiatives.

This is a very easy source of funds, and there is a way to make it easier. If you have a brother on the inside of the organization, or if you have a faculty member with pull that can help your cause, you stand a better chance of receiving funding. Also, if you can get another organization to partner with you (especially if they have more pull than you do) you stand an even better chance of getting the money you request.

There is free money out there – you just have to be eager enough to ask for it.

Fraternity Raffle

Potential Profit: $10,000++

Planning Required: Low

Partner Recommended: No

This might be the best fundraising idea because it is very easy, and very profitable. If your fraternity doesn't have a raffle each semester, then you are leaving a lot of money on the table.

I knew an organization that had 100 members, and each year they raffled off a Harley Davidson motorcycle. Each member was required to sell 20 raffle tickets. Each ticket was $10.

If you do the math, 20 tickets at $10 is $200 per member. $200 per member times 100 members means that they sold $20,000 in tickets. The Harley cost $10,000, and the organization put $10,000 in their pocket.

Your chapter doesn't have to do anything that big, but the possibility is there.

The average chapter size is around 50 brothers. Let's say that each brother is responsible for selling 10 tickets at $10 a pop. He can sell them to his girlfriend, his parents, his grandma, his dog – it doesn't matter. But he is responsible for selling 10. Keep in mind that there are always going to be those couple of brothers who sell way more than 10, but that isn't expected or required.

If each brother can do the minimum, then the fundraiser will gross $5000.

However, there needs to be a prize, and this is a very critical component. Right now, an iPad would be the perfect raffle item. The cheapest one is only $500. That means the chapter would net $4500.

And there is no reason not to do this each semester. Again, this is very minimal effort, and huge financial benefit for the chapter.

Fraternity/Sorority Date Auction

Potential Profit: $2000+

Planning Required: High

Partner Recommended: Yes

Partner with a sorority to have a date auction as a philanthropy. All the proceeds will be split between the sorority's charity of choice and the fraternity's charity of choice.

The setup requires a lot of leg work, and because of this it is good to have a partner organization.

First, reserve an auditorium on campus for the auction. That will be fairly simple and straight forward.

Then, decide how many people you plan on auctioning off. Some of the brothers and sisters will not want to be auctioned off for several reasons. Maybe they have a boyfriend or girlfriend. Maybe they are shy and don't want to be on stage in front of a group of people. Regardless, don't put them in a situation where they are uncomfortable.

Once the chapters figure out how many of their members they are going to auction off (should be 20 to 30 depending on the size of the event), it is time to plan the actual dates.

For the dates, the brothers and sisters need to solicit local businesses for donations. For their donations, the businesses will be prominently mentioned when their date is auctioned off, and their logo will appear on all promotional items for the event. This will be great exposure for those businesses and cheap advertising.

Promoting the event is important. Everyone on campus should know about it. You should be able to work out a deal with the school paper to print an ad about the event. The event is for charity, and they will want to promote the positive things that are happening on campus.

The paper will also probably print an actual article about the event both before and after if someone actually writes it for them. Don't miss out on this great opportunity.

In addition, don't forget to announce it to the Greek Community. Mention it at Panhellenic meeting, NPH and IFC meeting. Also, mail a formal invitation to each chapter on campus inviting them to attend the event.

Finally, print T-shirts that advertise the event. Having both the sorority and fraternity wear these shirts the week before the event will be great to get the word out.

On the night of the actual event, be sure the MC has clever write-ups on each person who is going to be auctioned off. And then have fun!

This is a way to earn an easy couple thousand dollars for charity. As you can see, the planning portion of this event is pretty involved. To be done well will require a lot of interaction between the sorority and fraternity. And that should build the type of friendships and lasting relationships that will greatly benefit the fraternity in the long run.

Golf Tournament Fundraiser

Potential Profit: $2500+

Planning Required: High

Partner Recommended: No

Having a golf tournament as a fundraiser is a way to have a great time and fundraise a lot money for the fraternity.

You will first need to find a course to host the tournament. Find the cheapest local course you can find. Remember, it is a fundraiser. Keep your expenses minimal.

Next you will need to find people to play in the tournament. You need to create a buzz with your alumni. If you can get one or two influential alumni to take interest in the event, often they can convince others. Also, invite friends and family to the event. You really don't care who plays, as long as a lot of people do.

Several days before the tournament you should have a good head count. Say you charge $25 over what the course charges you. Take a portion of that and buy prizes. Do not focus on golf prizes either. Most people who will be playing probably won't be golfers and won't be interested in a dozen balls.

Once you get people signed up, it is time to focus on making serious money off this thing. Solicit sponsors for each green, fairway and tee on the course. There should be 54 sponsors total.

Contact your local Kinkos to have signs made to place on the course. Make it everyone's responsibility to find sponsors. If you have 50 brothers, that is less than one sponsor per brother. The brother can have their grandmother be a sponsor, or an alum they are close with. They can have their Dad's business or the local college bar become a sponsor.

Charge whatever you think a reasonable rate is that they will pay. If you charge $25 a sponsor (which is super cheap) then that will bring in $1350. Take out $150 in expenses to make signs and you have a profit of $1200. That is a good return for minimal effort.

On tournament day, don't forget to sell mulligans and red ball busters. A mulligan is a do-over and a red ball buster is an opportunity to hit from the girls tees. Offer this option for a minimum of $5 a pop. That will net you a quick hundred or two.

Don't forget to sell shirts for the event. A nice polo with a logo can be had for a relatively cheap price. Have the participants pre-order, so the fraternity doesn't have to front the money and get stuck with the leftovers.

All in all – you can turn a simple event into a serious fundraiser. And everyone will have a good time in the process.

Cow Chip Bingo Fundraiser

Potential Profit: $2000+

Planning Required: Medium

Partner Recommended: Yes

The cow chip fundraiser isn't the highlight of this event – just the revenue source.

First off, plan a fun, country-style event. Have a concert, huge bonfire and hay rides. You want to make it a large enough draw where you will have no problems getting people to attend.

The event should happen where there is a field roped off and marked out with 500 squares. Each square is numbered.

Charge a $10 admission to the event. In exchange for the admission, the person will get a square on the field. Give them the option to buy other squares as well.

Put a cow in the field, and the first square he dumps in is the winner. The winner will get $1000.

If you can sell the 500 squares, then the fraternity will end up with a $4000 profit. However, if you have a partner you will have to split the proceeds. You will also have to pay for the band. In all though, making $2000 on this event should not be that hard.

Again, notice that success is easier when you combine a fun event with the fundraiser. Focus on having fun, and then profiting from that fun. This is the easiest way to fundraise.

Haunted House Fundraiser

Potential Profit: $2000+

Planning Required: Medium

Partner Recommended: Yes

I'll be perfectly honest, I would not pay to visit a haunted house. I personally don't see the appeal. However, there are tons of people that do.

Because of that, there is a lot of potential for an awesome fundraiser. If done right, it is also an opportunity to have a great time.

For the set up, you first need to find a place to have the event. I don't recommend doing it at the chapter house. It would be fantastic if there was a place on campus that you can use. This will be the hardest part of the set up.

Once you find the place, work on making it scary. Google "scary haunted houses" and you will get literally hundreds of great ideas. Make it as scary as possible. Remember your audience will be college students, and you want the news to travel by word of mouth.

It is a good idea to partner with a sorority with this project. This will help with the promotion, but also make it a lot more fun for the brothers.

As with any fundraiser, promotion will be key. Be sure that shirts are made, and that the brothers and sisters are wearing them the few weeks before the event. Be sure you are using your social networks to publicize the event.

As for making a profit – let's assume you run the house for four nights and get 100 people each night. If you charge $5 a head, that is an easy $2000. That is with a really low turnout. You have the ability to get a couple hundred people per night. That would mean huge profits for your chapter.

Hay Maze Fundraiser

Potential Profit: $4500+

Planning Required: Medium

Partner Recommended: No

Maybe it is the redneck in me showing, but hay mazes are a lot of fun for kids.

First, find a local farmer to 'rent' you bails of hay for a few weeks. Hopefully, you'll have someone in your chapter that has a connection that can help.

Then, find a field to have the event. It is best to have the event somewhere where there is a lot of drive-by traffic. This will serve as free advertising. Be sure to put up a huge sign that entices kids to come.

Once you do that, set up the maze. Remember not to make it too difficult, but not too easy either. The last thing you want is a kid to be stuck in the maze for hours. You want to churn these kids through the maze, because more kids means more money.

Also at the event, be sure that you are maximizing your fundraising potential. Sell hot chocolate, kettle popcorn, snow cones or cotton candy. If you can make your destination a fun place for the kids, the parents will always spend a few extra bucks to make their kids happier.

As for profit - let's say you do the fundraiser for two weekends. That is four days. If your location is good, you should easily be able to get 200 kids through a day. That is $4000. You should also be able to make $500 selling 'other' stuff.

All in all, this is a pretty simple fundraiser with minimal effort.

Bowling Tournament Fundraiser

Potential Profit: $1600+

Planning Required: low

Partner Recommended: No

This might be the easiest fundraiser there is. It should be criminal if your fraternity doesn't do this.

First off, contact a local bowling ally and reserve the place one night. You should be able to arrange it where each person can bowl three games and get shoes for a discounted price.

Then, create a trophy for the winning team. Mount an old bowling pin on a base and you have your trophy. Be sure to add the names of the winners to the base every time you have the tournament.

Then, charge $80 per team ($20 per man) to enter the tournament. This should leave about $40 of profit for the fraternity for each team.

If you can get 20 teams to the event, that is $800 profit. Don't forget to do this event every semester.

It is fantastically simple, and turns an awesome brotherhood event into a great fundraiser.

Cardboard Boat Race Fundraiser

Potential Profit: $1600+

Planning Required: low

Partner Recommended: No

If you have never seen a cardboard boat race, you are missing out. These are a ton of a lot of fun, and are very easy to set up.

The idea is fairly straight forward. The participants will have to construct a boat made of cardboard, glue and duct tape. They will use lots of duct tape. The oar needs to be constructed of the same material. All participants need to wear life vests for safety.

The winner of the race will be the boat who crosses the finish line first. You can also give out prizes for best design or funniest design, but I think that only complicates things. Most boats will sink, but that will lead to a lot of laughs and entertainment for all.

As with all fundraisers, advertising is the key. Hopefully, you will be able to get each fraternity on campus to sponsor a boat. Also, be sure to advertise it with the dorm councils, service organizations and academic groups on campus. With a little bit of effort, you should be able to find 50 participants pretty easy.

If you charge $25 a boat, that is $1250 raised. If you give out $250 as the prize, then the fraternity can pocket $1000. That isn't a bad return on a very simple event.

Dog Wash Fundraiser

Potential Profit: $1000+

Planning Required: Low

Partner Recommended: No

I hate washing my dog. I like the little guy, and even don't mind when he decides to sleep in my bed. However, I absolutely hate washing him, and I choose to pay someone $40 a month to wash him and give him a haircut.

The problem with that is there is no need to give him a haircut every month. I just need him to get his monthly bath. However, I am too lazy to actually do it.

That is where a fantastic fundraising opportunity lies.

If your fraternity would have a dog wash fundraiser, you can make a bunch of money fast.

The setup is similar to setting up a car wash. You just need a water source, soap, towels and a good location. Set up where people commonly walk their dogs. This will get you maximum exposure.

Charge $10 per dog, but realize most people will give you more. If you can wash 100 dogs, that is $1000. Not a bad fundraiser.

Rubber Ducky Fundraiser

Potential Profit: $750+

Planning Required: Low

Partner Recommended: No

This is another very simple fundraiser that takes very minimal setup.

Sell tickets for the fundraiser. Sell them cheap – either $2 a piece or 3 for $5. Each ticket will correspond with a number on a rubber duck.

On race day, send all the ducks down a river. The first duck to the finish line is the winner, as is the person with the corresponding ticket.

Rubber ducks are pretty cheap. You can get a dozen for less than $4. If you buy 50 dozen (600 ducks) you will end up spending $200. If you can sell those ducks for $2 a pop, you gross $1000.

However, you have to give a prize to the winner. Give out something in the $200 to $300 range, and you have a decent fundraiser that should net $750.

Mardi Gras Fundraiser

Potential Profit: $1000+

Planning Required: Low

Partner Recommended: No

Sometimes the best ideas are the simplest. Every year, craziness ensues in New Orleans for Mardi Gras. A fraternity would be foolish not to tap into this fantastic theme that has become the stuff of legend.

The set-up is quite simple. Buy a bunch of beads and give each brother a share. Sell beads at the event for $1 each. The fraternity should be able to make an easy several hundred bucks at the party by selling beads.

Be sure to give the brothers beads that are nicer and more distinctive from the beads the chapter sells to outsiders. You want it to be very noticeable if a guest has beads from a brother or from somewhere else.

Then, announce to everyone that at midnight that the girl with the most beads will be honored as this year's bead queen. Explain that beads from a brother count double or triple the other beads. Put together a prize for the winner.

After that, sit back and enjoy the party. Be sure to have a count down every hour to encourage people to gather beads. This will be a great time for everyone and a fantastic fundraiser.

Dorm Storm Fundraiser

Potential Profit: $1000+

Planning Required: Low

Partner Recommended: No

One night, a few of us were sitting at the chapter house. A brother came up and said that he and the new member class were going to have a fundraiser for our chapter philanthropy. He asked if any of us wanted to participate.

Of course, we agreed. The brother's idea was to storm the dorm asking for donations to our charity. There was one caveat though – we would only accept loose change. We wouldn't accept dollar bills.

So we broke into two man teams, and we stormed the dorms for about an hour. After, we met at the chapter house and had nearly $1000 in change for our charity.

This is a very simple idea, but extremely profitable.

Car Wash Fundraiser

Potential Profit: $1000+

Planning Required: Low

Partner Recommended: No

This one is the oldest one in the book, but there is a reason it is included. It works!

The setup is simple. Just find a place which will donate water and let you have your car wash. Buy some soap and you have a great fundraiser.

Be sure that you have adequate signage for your event. Be sure that you are near a busy road so you can maximize your visibility.

In my opinion, it is better to ask for a donation instead of a fee for the car wash. Have your sign say "You Name the Price". You will normally get about $10 for each wash.

If you can wash 100 cars, you should earn a quick $1000. Not bad for an afternoon's work.

BBQ Fundraiser

Potential Profit: $5000+

Planning Required: High

Partner Recommended: No

A fraternity at my school had a great idea. They held Pig Stock (a play on Woodstock). Pig Stock was a huge pig pickin'— a barbeque for those of you not from the south.

The setup was simple. They found an open field where they could have the event. They built a stage and hired a couple local bands to play. They put some tables out for people to eat and made the event BYOB. It was a very simple setup.

The genius of their plan was in their marketing. They sold tickets on campus for weeks prior to the event. This served as great publicity, and ensured they received their money early. The brothers in the fraternity regularly wore T shirts promoting the event. They created a hype and an aura around the event that pretty much guaranteed its success.

If my memory serves me correct, the tickets cost $10 each. I don't think there were a thousand people there, but there were definitely several hundred. The fraternity made an easy $5000 that day, probably much more. And everyone had a fantastic time in the process.

Fishing Tournament Fundraiser

Potential Profit: $3000+

Planning Required: Med

Partner Recommended: No

Fishermen are among the greatest people in the world, and also the most competitive. There is a core group of fishermen in every area who live for fishing tournaments. That creates a fantastic fundraising opportunity.

The beauty of this event is it is a simple event to plan and execute.

The typical tournament will take registrations before the event. Charge $100 for each boat which consists of two men.

To find participants, fish where the fish are! Put flyers up at the local sportsman stores and bait shops. Go online and try to find local message boards about fishing.

The morning of the event start everyone off at the same time. End the tournament at noon, and have a weigh in.

The winner is the boat with the most weight among a certain number of fish. You will have to check your local gaming laws to see what number that should be. You should also give a prize for 2nd and 3rd place.

If you give $400 to the winner, $200 for 2nd and $100 for 3rd, you should have sweetened the pot enough to get a good turnout. If you can get 30 boats out, you will be able to raise $2300 from entrance fees.

Also, don't forget to ask for sponsors. Surely you will be able to get some of the local sportsman stores and bait shops to help sponsor the event. This should net another $500 pretty easy.

Finally, don't forget to have someone grill up burgers and dogs and serve lunch during the weigh in. The guys will be hungry after being on the water all morning, and will want lunch. If there are 60 guys, you should be able to make at least another $200.

All in all, this is a very easy fundraiser to pull off and it is very profitable.

NCAA March Madness Fundraiser

Potential Profit: $280+

Planning Required: Low

Partner Recommended: No

This is a very, very easy fundraiser. Essentially, you are using the NCAA basketball tournament for a raffle fundraiser.

In March, sell each team in the NCAA tournament for $10 in a blind draw. There are 68 teams total, meaning you will gross $680.

Give the person who draws the winner $400 – and the fraternity pockets the $280.

Again, this is a super easy fundraiser which also makes watching the tournament a lot more fun for the brothers.

Use these ideas to make your chapter finances strong and be sure to use the funds wisely. Think about your biggest issues in the fraternity (recruitment, cost of dues, housing) and think of how you can use the additional funds to become more successful in those areas.

You can use a strong fundraising program as a spring board to your chapter's success.

8 – HOW TO WIN YOUR CHAPTER ELECTION

If you are reading this book, then there is a good chance that you want to run for office in your fraternity. Below is a step-by-step guide which will help you determine if you are a viable candidate, and how to get elected if you are.

Have you earned the right to run?

Before you can learn how to win your fraternity election, you must figure out if you have earned the right to run.

The truth is, a lot of people want to be the president of their fraternity. They believe that this title will make them a leader. These types of brothers really don't understand what leadership is all about.

You cannot become a leader by simply having that title. Respect and recognition must be earned, and the only way to earn it is through your actions.

In my chapter, the leader of our fraternity was not the president. Truth is, he never even sat on the executive board. When he spoke though, brothers listened. The brotherhood would follow him anywhere, and would look for his approval on issues. He was our true leader, even if he was never elected to that role.

Why did he have that respect? For one, his actions were always in line with the ideals of our fraternity. He was willing to put the hard work in to making our fraternity great, and the brothers respected his efforts. He was charismatic, and the brothers like being around him.

On the flip side, he didn't do things to embarrass the fraternity. Think about it, do you really want your fraternity president to be a drunk guy at parties? Do you want your president to be the guy who disrespects women? Do you want him to be the guy who is always looking to pick a fight? Do you want him to be the guy that thinks drugs are more important than school work?

My guess is no...

Remember that this is going to be the brother who represents your chapter for an entire year. That is 25% of the average brother's college experience. A guy that is an embarrassment should never be elected.

It is more than that though. Life would be a lot simpler if the only qualification for office was to not embarrass yourself or the chapter. The president has to be a cut above the rest of the brothers. He gets that way by how he presents himself.

A brother who would have earned the right to run would be someone who is clean-cut and well-spoken. This person is going to be the face of the organization. While some will argue that looks don't matter, without a doubt they do.

This brother is going to be dealing with the university, IFC, sororities and the national headquarters. Think about the difference in their reaction if they meet a brother who is neatly groomed, wearing a pressed shirt and pants as opposed to a brother who has dirty, long hair and wrinkled clothes. How you look makes a difference.

It is also important that this brother is well-spoken. Not only will he be responsible for addressing the chapter each week during the chapter meeting, but he will also be responsible for interacting with those organizations I mentioned earlier. If the brother cannot communicate, he will never be respected as a leader. This means that he will have to be able to get his point across clearly and succinctly.

If the brother has met those criteria, he still isn't fully qualified.

The next question that needs to be answered is does this brother have the experience necessary to lead the organization? If the brother is newly initiated, in nearly every case the answer is no. The president should be a brother at least a year before he runs for office.

I am sure you will agree that this logic makes a lot of sense. How can you run a chapter if you just got initiated and haven't fully experienced fraternity life yet?

That being said, I am always fearful of making these types of blanket statements. There will be examples of brothers who become president early in their fraternity experience who became quite successful. Often, these men take over chapters in distress, and are able to lead a turnaround. These guys are the exceptions to the rule though. This situation should be avoided if at all possible.

Finally, have you earned the trust of your brothers? It won't matter how you present yourself and how much experience you have if the brothers don't trust you.

If you have met these criteria, then you have earned the right to think about running for president. This right will just put you in the conversation. There is still a long way to go before you will get elected...

Do you understand the needs of the brothers?

It is pretty easy to put a campaign together based on the things *you* want. However, that isn't what a leader does. To lead effectively, you must focus on the needs of your followers, and receive satisfaction when they get what *they* want.

Understand though, that if you are the right person for the job, their needs are going to overlap with yours. If they don't, you must seriously question if you are the right person for the job.

Most aspiring leaders will think they have it figured out at this point. They know their brothers like to party, and they know they like girls. They figure if they can focus on those two things, they are a shoe-in to be elected.

Think about what that says for your fraternity though. Sure, parties and girls are fun, but is that really what you are all about?

Fraternity is so much more than that. A good leader needs to open the brotherhood's eyes to the opportunities outside the norm.

Below is a list of a few of the desires that the brothers of a strong fraternity have:

Academic Success – Going to college is about getting an education right? A strong chapter will have brothers that are dedicated to their studies. The brothers will be thrilled if the fraternity can help them achieve academic success.

Social Excellence – I know I just discounted parties, but the social scene is an important part of the life of a fraternity man. Your brothers want to be a part of a vibrant social scene, and they are looking for a leader to get them there.

Meet Girls – Again, I know I just discounted girls, but let's face facts. Your brothers are probably thinking about them 95% of the time. This is probably pretty high on their priorities list. Remember though, this isn't limited to meeting new girls and being popular with the girls on campus. It is also about making the fraternity a great place for the girlfriends of brothers. While no brother with a long-term girlfriend will ever admit to it, this is something that they all secretly desire. If you make your chapter accommodating to girlfriends, you will have happier brothers as a result.

Develop Leadership – Men join fraternities for a lot of reasons. One of the best reasons is to develop leadership. There is no other type of organization on campus that has such a wide range of responsibility with such little oversight. This appeals to your brothers. Brothers will look for a leader who can develop their leadership abilities and give them opportunities to grow.

Give Back to the Community – This is one of the core values of every fraternity. It is the duty of the more fortunate to provide for the less fortunate. However, this does not work if it is forced. The brothers will give back, but you must make it something they want to do, instead of something they have to do.

Improve the Chapter House – Brothers take pride in their chapter house. Developing initiatives towards improving the house will go a long way in improving the morale of the brotherhood.

The Fraternity's Image on Campus – Everyone wants to be liked and popular. Sometimes though, the brothers don't know how to make this happen. They are looking for a leader to show them the way.

Reduce Dues – This is a natural one. No one wants to pay more money for anything. If a leader can figure out how to provide more with less, then that leader will become an attractive candidate.

Future Employment Opportunities – The point for many brothers in going to college is to enable them to get good jobs. Your fraternity probably has a huge network of alumni brothers to tap into for job opportunities. This is something that is very appealing to the brotherhood.

These are just some ideas, and in most cases the most obvious ones for most chapters. You are going to have to figure out what your chapter's problems are. Every chapter is unique. You can't lead the brotherhood unless you understand where they want to be led.

Being able to identify their issues is just a piece of the puzzle. Developing a solution is what separates the leaders from the complainers.

To become president or to win a fraternity election you need to be able to identify what issues the brothers have, and then come up with a way that you can lead them to a solution. If you can do that, then you probably have the right stuff to get elected.

Put together a platform

If you have made it to this step, then you have met the basic criteria of what your chapter is looking for in a president. You also have a good grasp on what issues your brothers are facing, and have solutions to address those issues. The next step is putting together a platform.

An effective platform is not one filled with visions of grandeur like the following statements:

- Make the Fraternity the Best on Campus
- Become the Most Popular Fraternity with Sororities
- Have the Best Parties
- Become the Coolest Guys on Campus

Those are all pretty awesome goals, but not much of a platform. The reason is it states the desired outcome, but not what the chapter has to do to get there.

The basis of your platform has to be the solutions you have for the chapter's problems. It is really as simple as that. The brothers have problems, and if you have the answers, you should get elected.

How you organize your platform is very important. Remember, a key part of being president is having the ability to communicate your vision to the rest of the chapter.

Organize your platform on a single sheet of paper – never more than one sheet. Explain your goal, then what you are going to do to get there. It should be goal, bullet point, bullet point, bullet point. There is no need to write long paragraphs. If you do that, you will lose the brothers in the details.

Also, you need to focus your efforts. Listing 20 problems that you are going to solve is too ambitious. Pick the top five or six, and then go with it.

Discuss your platform with the brotherhood

Now that you have your platform, you need to pitch it to the brothers. Doing this step right is what will enable you to win if you are in the middle of a close election.

This is probably the most difficult and time-consuming of all the steps. It is your responsibility to discuss your platform with each and every brother. The reason you did not go into great detail in your written platform is because you are going to tell the brothers as much detail as they want in person.

For this to work though, you must be prepared. You must be able to speak in-depth about each one of your points. This means that you will have had to do your homework, and you have spent time thinking about what you are trying to accomplish. You can't get caught not understanding your own initiatives. That is the fastest way to lose credibility.

Without a doubt you will have a brother who will disagree with everything you say. There are a few of those guys in every chapter (unfortunately). When you talk to that guy, and he attempts to punch bullets in your platform, sit there and take his abuse.

Then, become excited and tell him you are glad he brought up those points. They are very valid, and would he take some time brainstorming how to solve those issues?

This brother is just looking for a reason to complain. If you can flip that back on him and make him part of the solution, you can turn this into a win/win for both of you.

The beauty of this step is that if you have a proper perspective on the issues, the brothers will be excited about what you are telling them. They will get behind you. Most importantly, they will discuss your proposals with the other brothers when you aren't there, almost like they are campaigning for you.

This is how I won my election for IFC president. I had discussed my platform with the chapter representatives who I knew would be voting in the election. We went into great detail about the platform, and I explained how it would benefit their chapter.

My opponent, even though he was a great guy and leader of his fraternity, did nothing of the sort.

After we gave our election speeches and left the room, there was an open discussion about our candidacies. Two of the most influential guys in the room had bought into my platform during our discussion, and eagerly supported me during this discussion. While I wasn't there to confirm this, I am pretty confident that this is what got me elected.

There are a couple additional points to remember in this step.

First, never bad-mouth your opponent. You can disagree with an opponent, but it is never acceptable to trash him behind his back. This is especially true because he is your brother. These types of people rarely get ahead in life, and you don't want to be that type of guy. True leaders get ahead on their own merit, not by beating others down.

Second, never split your own vote. I once won an election because my opponent ran for president and vice-president. His thought was that if he didn't get one, at least he'd get the other and he'd be happy with either.

The problem with this theory is that it is flawed from the start. Some brothers are going to vote for you for president, some for vice, which means you essentially split your vote. Don't do anything stupid like that.

If you do this step, and do it well, your chances of getting elected go up exponentially.

Election Speech

This is where most brothers try to get elected. However, if you have done all the previous steps, this step really doesn't matter.

If I were in this position, I would stand up and say the following:

"First off, it is an honor to be a part of this discussion. I love our fraternity and everything we stand for, and it would be a great privilege to be elected to be your president.

I have spoke to each one of you about my plans if I get elected. Each one of you has my promises to you and the chapter. As you know, I am a man of my word, and accomplishing those goals will be my absolute priority.

In addition, I hope you see the effort and passion I put into my platform and the potential of my ideas. I will be a leader who will not rest until we accomplish these objectives.

Finally, I am asking for your vote. I would like the opportunity to lead our chapter next year, and make it the best chapter on campus."

Something like that is short, simple, and to the point. The brotherhood already has your campaign promises (bring additional copies to give out the night of the election). They know what you are all about, because you have taken the time to discuss it with them. There is no need to belabor the points, because they already have them.

If there is a question and answer session, be prepared for the questions. You should be able to guess what questions are going to be asked, so prepare for them. Never put yourself in front of an audience in any situation unprepared if you can avoid it.

Deliver on your promises!

If you have done the previous five steps, you should get elected.

Being president is one of the most rewarding experiences you can have as a fraternity brother. You will be responsible for starting the next 100 years of traditions, or protecting the previous 100 years of traditions – or both!

It is an awesome responsibility and feeling when the chapter looks to you for answers because you are the guy with the gavel.

The new members that you initiate as president will always look at you as the president of the fraternity, because you will be the one who brought them into it. That is a special honor.

There is an experience that is even more rewarding than being president.

If you have done all five steps, you will have presented yourself as a man your chapter can be proud of. You will have shown that you have the passion for improving your chapter, and you have the motivation to make sure the brotherhood has the same desire. You will have presented your vision in a way that brings honor to both you and your chapter.

In short, you will have become a fraternity leader – a title that is earned. This is much more valuable and important than any title that can be won by a vote.

So if you have followed these steps – well done. You have already won, regardless of how the election turns out.

9 – THE 5 SECRETS OF FRATERNITY LEADERSHIP

In my experiences, there are five lessons you must learn in order to become an effective leader. I hope they help you as you develop your leadership style. I know I would have been a much better leader if someone would have shared these lessons with me when I was an undergrad.

The true beauty of these lessons is that they will not only help you become a great fraternity leader, but that you will be able to utilize these lessons in life after college. They will help form the foundation which will make you very successful in your professional and personal life.

Lesson #1 – It isn't about you – it's about the brotherhood!

This is tough for most fraternity leaders to accept. After all, you are going to be the one who does most of the work for the chapter. It would be natural to want some of the recognition for all of your effort.

This was a tough one for me to grasp. Normally, when you see a guy who has won as many awards as I did, and a guy who served two years as chapter president (which is always a bad idea), you will find a guy who might have been able to share the spotlight a little more.

That isn't to say that I didn't work my tail off for my chapter or that my chapter didn't have some great accomplishments – we did. However, I seemed to always be the one recognized when we succeeded. This limited my effectiveness as a leader.

The strange thing is if I would have deflected more of the praise I received to my chapter, that probably would have been the motivation needed to achieve even greater things. We would have all received more recognition as a result.

Remember that to lead is to serve, and to serve you must remember that it isn't about you. It is about the brothers in the chapter. If you do a good job, recognition will come in the future.

One of the easiest ways to make it about the brotherhood is to make sure they get the credit for chapter accomplishments.

When I was IFC president, I had a great community service idea that would also promote Greek Life in our community. We raised over $5,000 that we were going to donate to the Jimmy V foundation for Cancer Research.

One of my VP's knew someone in the athletic department, and thought he could arrange for us to make the presentation at a basketball game. That meant even more positive publicity for Greek Life, and I was all for it.

We were offered to make the presentation at halftime of the NC State vs. Duke game to Jim Valvano's wife. I was excited about the opportunity, until I realized that I would not be the one making the presentation. They had asked my VP if he would make the presentation on our behalf.

I hate to admit, but I was a little disappointed that I wouldn't be making the presentation. It was my idea, and I was the president. Wasn't it my role to be the figurehead? It would have been an incredible experience, a real honor, to have made that presentation.

I had to remember that it wasn't about me though, it was about the organization I was leading. I swallowed my pride, and acted happy that my VP would have that honor.

In hindsight, that turned out to be a blessing in disguise.

The VP and I would become great friends, and to this day he would do anything in the world for me. I think the foundation for that friendship happened with this event.

The rest of the leadership team recognized what happened, and worked harder for me as a result. Everyone involved in the event knew that it was my idea. They thought more highly of me because I did not hog the spotlight. This helped me with future projects.

Most importantly, the IFC under my leadership was able to make a significant contribution to cancer research, something we all were very proud of.

Another way to make it about the brotherhood is to be sure you recognize excellence.

As a matter of fact, I would probably not have remained involved with Greek Life as an alumnus if someone didn't take the time to recognize me. Years ago, I was selected to be the recipient of Pi

Lambda Phi's Rafer Johnson Achievement Award at our national convention.

My parents were invited to the awards banquet. They were able to witness one of the most special moments of my life. Neither one of them was Greek, and still don't understand my bond with the fraternity. It meant the world to me that they were able to see how important the fraternity was in my life. It was an experience I'll never forget.

Because someone took the time to recognize me with this award, I have spent countless hours trying to give back to the Greek Community.

You can do the same thing for the brothers in your chapter. Your brothers will do some amazing things in the span of a year. There are hundreds of ways to recognize their achievement. The beauty is when you recognize excellence, it inspires greatness in others as well. Be a leader who creates an environment of high achievement, and promote excellence.

A final way to make the fraternity about the brotherhood, and probably the most important way, is by saying thank you often.

People like compliments and they like to be appreciated. The two most powerful words are 'thank you'.

When I graduated from NC State, I got a job with an Italian robotics company. This was a dream job for a young guy. I was able to travel the world, spending a good portion of my time in a small town in the Italian Alps. I was paid really well to work with pretty interesting technology – laser guided robots. It really was a fantastic first job.

A few months after I was hired I asked my boss why he hired me. I knew there were hundreds of applicants for the job. I expected him to make note of my leadership experiences in the fraternity, and say that that is what separated me from my peers.

What he told me was very surprising. He said that I was hired because I had taken the time to write a thank you note. He said that he had scores of qualified applicants, but I seemed sincere in my note, and he appreciated the gesture.

Taking 30 seconds to say thank you landed me a dream job. That shows you the power those two simple words have.

If you are a motivated leader with a big agenda, you are going to need guys to help you make your dreams a reality. This won't be possible if your brothers don't feel appreciated. Take the time to say thank you often, and the more publicly the better.

If you do these things, your chapter will become stronger and more motivated. Brothers will become eager to make a difference, because they will know that they will be recognized for their efforts. They will know the chapter is about them.

Lesson 2 - Handle Adversity with Class

You will have trying moments as a fraternity leader. Things don't always go as planned. I hope you have those times.

Now I don't hope you have them because I want you to struggle; just the opposite. How you handle adversity will define you as a leader.

Think about it – it is easy to lead when times are good. Anyone can be a leader during those times.

The true test is during those trying times. Those times when the answer isn't easy, and puts your character to the test.

So I hope you have those times, because you will grow from those experiences. You will look back and remember the tough calls you made, and you will be proud that you had the courage and conviction to stand up for what is right.

I'll tell you something, some brothers will not be happy with the decisions you make. If you make those decisions in accordance to your values and your fraternity's values though, they will respect you for it.

I want to share with you a story of how I had to cope with trying times.

I was in the Air Force and my first deployment was to Iraq. My deployment team consisted of 157 Airmen. I was either directly or indirectly responsible for all of them.

We were mortared nearly every day. The weather was ridiculous. The work environment was as stressful as it gets, and we were away from our families for six long months.

I went over there and I was going to get the most out of my experience. I believed, and still do believe, in what we are doing over there. I was going to make a difference.

I started volunteering at the medical facility on base. At this location soldiers who were injured in the field would wait to be transported out of Iraq.

I just showed up one day and asked how I could help. I spent most of my time talking to bored soldiers as they waited for their planes.

However, I spent so much time over there that people actually thought I was a nurse. They even asked me to give IVs.

Through that experience I witnessed the horror of war. I saw six young female marines who were burned almost beyond recognition by a car bomb in Fallujah. If there is anything worse in life than being burned, I don't want to know about it. I can't describe how terrible that was.

I have also brushed the teeth of a guy who had both of his arms blown off by an IED. I have helped a guy call his mother, because he couldn't get a hold of her to tell her that he had just lost a leg in combat.

That is how I spent my free time.

The most amazing thing happened though. My guys started noticing how I was spending my free time, and decided to join me.

I never asked them to help, and wouldn't have thought less of them if they didn't come out. They worked their tails off, and needed their downtime. Every night they started showing up to help, often staying until three and four in the morning.

It was also amazing how word spread. The squadron back home found out what we were doing, and wanted to help too. They ended up sending about $25,000 worth of supplies in care packages to the medical facility for the wounded soldiers.

On one particularly memorable night I was talking to a Marine who had been out in the field for a few months. I asked him if there was anything I can do for him or get for him. Sheepishly, he said he hadn't had anything but MREs for months, and he'd love to have a cheeseburger.

The other guys around us overheard the conversation and agreed that a burger sounded great.

So I got my guys together, there were about 20 of us that night, and we pooled together our cash. We had a Burger King on base and we sent the youngest guy to get as many burgers as he could. He got the burgers, and passed them out to the injured soldiers.

I sat back and watched. That night was better than 100 Christmases. I have never been so proud to be a leader...

My guys witnessed how I was handling this difficult situation, and even though they weren't asked, they were inspired to follow my lead and to do what they could to help. This is one of the most fantastic memories I have.

Now, I realize the tragedy of war is on the far end of the adversity spectrum. However, the point is just the same. You will have trying times as a leader in your fraternity and in your college career. How you handle that adversity is how you will be remembered and how you will grow as a leader.

Remember to always take the high road, even though it might not be the easiest thing to do. That is how you become respected, and how you become a leader of men.

Lesson 3 - Recruit Your Brothers – Not Strangers

Fraternities go about recruitment all wrong. It amazes me how much time, money and effort we waste trying to convince strangers to join our chapters, but we completely neglect doing the same thing for our brothers to make sure they stay.

You need to focus on recruiting the brothers you already have if you want your chapter to grow and become strong.

This became very apparent to me in a conversation I had with an undergraduate brother last summer. His chapter was having difficulty recruiting new members, and I offered to give him some tips to help.

The first thing I asked him is why should someone join his chapter?

He told me because his chapter was different than the rest of the fraternities on campus. That the brothers weren't typical 'frat guys'. He said that the brotherhood is especially close. In short, he gave me the same fluff answers that every chapter gives their rushees.

So I probed a little deeper and asked him what type of things the chapter does and what he is looking forward to. He said that the chapter throws a couple parties a year and is active in their philanthropy.

This brother really couldn't give me a compelling reason why someone should join his chapter. There was nothing he was pumped up about. Nothing he could brag on. Nothing he was excited to tell me.

Like I said though, this has nothing to do with recruitment. It has everything to do with the health of the chapter. If the brothers don't have a reason to be excited about the chapter, then the chapter is going to be in big trouble.

Because of that it is essential that the leadership team focuses on recruiting the brothers who are already in the chapter.

When you plan your semester and year – please don't forget this lesson.

So how do you recruit your chapter? Like I explained in the finance chapter, you need to give the brothers good value for their dues. If you expect them to pay up to several hundred dollars a semester, then it is reasonable for them to expect to get a good return on their investment.

By good value, you obviously need to have great social events – fraternities are social organizations after all. That should be pretty obvious.

It needs to be more than that though. It really isn't hard to find a party on a college campus. You need to do something that distinguishes yourself from the crowd. You need to be able to give an example of something that you can do if you are in a fraternity, but can't do if you aren't.

I came up with a great idea when I was an undergrad at my fraternity's national convention. By chance, I sat with a few brothers from our Illinois chapter at dinner one night. They were bragging about how great they were, and I decided to call them on it. I told them that my chapter would like to have a road trip to visit their chapter in the fall, and come see for ourselves how great they really were.

They happily agreed to host us if we could make it out, but seriously doubted we would. After all, Raleigh, NC (where I went to school) is a long way from Champaign, IL.

I introduced the idea to my chapter, and everyone got behind it. To make a long story short, we ended up fundraising (and spending) $3500 for the trip.

We chartered a bus, and 22 of us made the trip to Illinois one long weekend. The Illinois guys were as great as they claimed, and were great hosts. It was a memorable experience that we still talk about when we get together years later.

The benefit of that weekend was huge. For those of us that went, those couple days turned into the highlight of the year. This event had a huge impact on our entire chapter operations for some time.

The brothers that went had an awesome story to tell – which had a huge impact on recruitment. Morale was high in the chapter, and the positive momentum from this weekend carried over into everything we did for a long time.

On the flip side, fraternities do a lot of things that really aren't a lot of fun or very productive – namely hazing.

Realize, though, that hazing doesn't typically kill a fraternity because it is illegal, it kills it because it destroys the chapter from the inside. It is death by a thousand cuts and a symptom of a chapter that isn't healthy.

Hazing isn't fun, and brothers aren't active in new member programs because of it. Outsiders are always watching what we do, and the type of guys we want will not join if they know they are going to be hazed. Worst of all, it pits brothers against brothers, which is exactly the opposite of what we are all about.

Am I saying that the new member programs shouldn't be challenging? Of course not. But you have the ability and creativity to make the new member nights challenging, educational, and a heck of a lot of fun.

If you can do that you will get a lot more participation from the brotherhood, and you'll have a lot fewer new members quitting the program. If you are creative enough – you can even make it a recruitment tool. All are huge wins for the chapter.

If you are reading this, you are probably one of the best and brightest guys in your fraternity. This is a serious problem that needs to be solved if we want Greek Life to survive.

The whole point about recruiting your brotherhood is to make the fraternity as much fun as you possibly can. If you do, your brothers will remain engaged in the chapter, and this will enable you to achieve your social, athletic, academic and philanthropic goals.

Lesson 4 – Get a little better each day

People fall in love with the home run idea, or home run event. However, the best way to improve, and make sure your improvements stick, is by a bunch of small improvements.

Take your typical chapter of about 50 guys. Imagine if each brother made it a point to do something to improve the chapter each day.

What they do doesn't have to be anything huge, and doesn't have to take more than a few minutes. For example, a brother could:

- Take the trash out at the house
- Eat dinner with a brother they haven't hung out with in a while
- Thank a brother for doing something (really anything)
- Help a brother prepare for an exam

You get the idea. If every brother makes it a point to do something that will make the fraternity better each day, it won't take long for your chapter to become truly special.

The reason for that is that there is a lot of power behind small wins. It creates momentum, which leads to bigger and better accomplishments. Your chapter will create a winning mentality, and the best part about it is every brother in the chapter will be a part of it.

Let me give you an example of how small wins can turn into significant accomplishments.

One day several of us were sitting around the chapter house when a brother showed up with the new member class. He said they had decided to have a fundraiser for our chapter philanthropy, and wanted to know if any of us wanted to help, which we of course agreed to.

The brother's idea was to go from dorm room to dorm room and ask for donations for our charity. However, we would not accept any bills, only change that the person may have lying around.

We broke into teams and spent an hour or two getting donations. After, we all met at the house.

The mountain of change we gathered was amazing. We ended up with close to a thousand dollars that we were proud to donate. Not bad for a few hours of effort.

While we did not intend to teach our new member class this lesson at the time, it showed them the power of accumulating small wins by a large group of people.

This is really true for all facets of life. If you want to make lasting improvement in anything – academics, finance, relationships, athletics – you do so by getting a little better every day.

This way your improvements will become habit, and become a way of life. That is how you will create a winning mentality with your brothers, and bring about lasting improvements in your chapter.

Lesson 5 – Be Dedicated to Lifelong Learning

If you want to be the leader – you have to strive to be the most knowledgeable person about the subject matter.

Let me give you an example. Let's say you and your three buddies are driving somewhere, and the car has a flat. Only one guy knows how to change the tire. Who becomes the leader in that situation? Obviously the guy who knows how to fix the tire...

It is more than just that though. How many times have we been around a person who knows how to change the tire, but for whatever reason doesn't have the drive to actually change it? So that is the formula. You have to have the knowledge, but you must also have the motivation to apply it.

Be sure to take advantage of talking to brothers from other chapters (both in your fraternity and outside). Every chapter out there does at least one thing really well. Learn what those are, and then bring it back to your chapter. Remember that you get one point in life for coming up with your own idea, but two points for copying someone else's.

Don't forget to utilize valuable resources like thefraternityadvisor.com. My site has literally hundreds of articles on all aspects of fraternity. This is a treasure trove of information for the motivated leader.

Also, take advantage of your alumni out there. Those that are active are that way because they truly believe in what your fraternity stands for, and they want to help you become as successful as possible. Don't let those valuable resources go untapped.

If you are lucky, then one of them will take you under their wing and help you in your fraternity experience.

I have been especially lucky because I have had two older, distinguished alumni from my fraternity mentor me. I wouldn't be the brother I am today without their guidance.

I want to share with you something that a mentor shared with me while I was in the military. A crusty old colonel sat a bunch of us young guys down and wanted to tell us what he thought the keys to leadership were. I would like to share them with you, because I think they are spot on.

He said that leadership really comes down to three shapes.

The first shape is a line. The line represents where you are in your organization. You must remember that there will always be people behind you and people in front of you on that line in your organization. You move further down the line by taking care of the people behind you – not the people in front of you.

Like I said in lesson 1 – it isn't about you, it's about the brotherhood. Take care of the brothers, and they will push you towards success.

The second shape was a triangle. The first corner represents you. The second corner represents your family. The third - your organization. If either one of those three gets out of whack, they will negatively impact the other two.

For you, your corners probably represent you, the fraternity and your academics. We have all seen 100 times where someone doesn't take care of themselves because of booze or drugs, and how that impacts the other facets of their life. We have also seen all too often a fantastic brother who did not meet their academic requirements, and that ruined the other two parts of their life. Be sure that you and the brothers under your leadership are maintaining this balance in life.

The third and final shape is a circle. The circle represents your circle of influence. We all have things we can control, and things we can't control. Focus on the things you can control, and don't waste time on the things you can't. Always be dedicated to making your circle the very best you can. Realize that all our circles overlap. If everyone makes their circle the very best they can, then you will really have a fantastic fraternity.

Remember this the next time you are at the house for a rush event or a new member event and certain brothers don't show up. You can't do anything about that, so don't worry about it. What you can do is focus on who is there, and making that event the very best it can be. That is what will ultimately make your organization stronger.

If you really want to be the best leader you can be, make the effort to become an expert on fraternity life. There are a ton of great resources out there just waiting for you to make the effort to utilize.

Someday you will be the guy with the flat. Make sure you know how to change the tire.

CONCLUSION

Before I finish the book, I want to explain why I am so passionate about this idea about becoming a great fraternity leader.

Let me tell a story….

I spent six months deployed to Balad, Iraq while I was in the Air Force. It was the summer of 2005.

My phone rang one morning.

On the other end was a nurse from the base hospital. She told me my fraternity brother Jim was hit by an IED last night, and was helicoptered in. The nurse said he needed to see me right away.

Now Jim and I were pretty tight. I was a year older, and was his RA his freshman year. We lived right across the hall from each other. Jim and I were and are diehard fraternity men . This formed a bond that can't be understood unless you have experienced it yourself.

He had joined the Army, and was deployed to Iraq the same time I was. We were hoping we would run into each other sometime during our deployment, but not under these circumstances.

After I hung up I got to the hospital as fast as I could. I was preparing myself for the worst. The nurse hadn't told me how he was, so I was prepared to see him missing an arm or a leg. I was petrified to see him.

I did a quick check when I first saw him. He had both his arms, and both his legs. What a relief.

It turned out the vehicle in front of him was hit by an IED. It killed the driver. He ran into that vehicle and had a severe concussion. On top of that, he was shaken up pretty bad because of the experience.

Now Jim is normally loud and ornery. Not this day though. I could tell he was shaken up. He gave me a big hug, and I could tell he was relieved to have me there.

I asked him what he needed. They had cut all his clothes off of him, and he needed a new uniform. I got that for him no problem.

What he really needed was something he didn't have to ask for. He needed a friend. He needed a brother to sit with him and help him through this traumatic experience.

That is what it is all about. That is why you want to be a great fraternity leader.

When your brother is in his most dire situation, and has no one else in the world to turn to, you want to be the one he can count on for help.

This was the most unexpected and most rewarding moment I have had as a brother in my fraternity.

Being a brother in a fraternity is not about parties, or new member events, or houses, or rush – it is about the most sincere form of friendship there is.

If you have the drive and dedication to give all you can to your fraternity, the fraternity will repay you many times over with amazing experiences and treasured friendships.

When you look back at your college experiences, you will not remember the everyday tasks of running your chapter. However, if you do those tasks well, it will reflect in your friendships. This will make the bonds you form with your brothers last a lifetime.

If you remember that, even if you forget everything else in this book, you will have the chance to be a pretty outstanding fraternity leader.

"Before you are a leader, success is all about growing yourself. When you become a leader, success is all about growing others."

-- Jack Welch

thefraternityadvisor.com

THANK YOU!

Thank you for reading my book. I hope it helps you grow as a leader and helps improve your chapter.

If you think The Fraternity Leader would help other fraternity men, please leave a review about the book on Amazon. I really appreciate it.

Also, be sure to check out my other books – The Chapter President and The Best of the Fraternityadvisor.com. Both are available on Amazon.

I wish you and your fraternity the very best.

Fraternally,
Pat

Made in the USA
San Bernardino, CA
29 January 2015